THE OFFICIAL
Democrats
ARE SUCH A
Joke Book

Compiled by Mike Hunt

All Rights Reserved

Copyright © 2011 by S&B Publishing

ISBN 978-1-4636019-9-7

First Printing – June 2011
Printed in the United States of America

www.AllAmericanBooks.com

D1418442

THE OFFICIAL DEMOCRATS ARE SUCH A JOKE BOOK

"If we want to save the whales, we call the Democrats. If we want to save the *world*, we call the Republicans." - Tom Adkins

PREFACE

If you really want to see humor in the Democrat way of thinking, you only need to look as far as the (accurate) way they are portrayed via satire. Take for instance the threats by liberals to leave the country if George W. Bush were to be re-elected President, and the laughs we were treated to when it actually happened. Their destination was naturally Canada, since it was both nearby and the recipient of many draft dodgers, and it was funny to imagine the flood of American liberals sneaking across the border into Canada as it sparked calls for increased Canadian patrols to stop the "illegal immigration." I'll let the "news" of the day take it from here.

The re-election of President Bush is prompting an exodus among left-leaning citizens who fear they'll soon be required to hunt, pray and agree with Bill O'Reilly. Canadian border farmers say it's not uncommon to see dozens of sociology professors, animal-rights activists and Unitarians crossing their fields at night.

"I went out to milk the cows the other day, and there was a Hollywood producer huddled in the barn," said Manitoba farmer Red Greenfield, whose acreage borders North Dakota. The producer was cold, exhausted and hungry. "He asked me if I could spare a latte and some free-range chicken, and when I said I didn't have any, he left. Didn't even get a chance to show him my screenplay!"

In an effort to stop the illegal aliens Greenfield erected higher fences, but the liberals scaled them, so he tried installing speakers that blare Rush Limbaugh monologues across the fields. "Not real effective," he said. "The liberals still got through, and Rush annoyed the cows so much they wouldn't give milk."

Officials are particularly concerned about smugglers who meet liberals near the Canadian border, pack them into Volvo station wagons, drive them across the border and leave them to fend for themselves. "A lot of them are not prepared for rugged conditions," an Ontario patrolman said. "I found one carload without a drop of drinking water. They did have a nice little Napa Valley cabernet, though."

When liberals are caught they're sent back across the border, often wailing loudly that they fear retribution from conservatives. Rumors have been circulating about the Bush administration establishing re-education camps in which liberals will be forced to drink domestic beer and watch NASCAR.

In the days since the election, liberals have turned to sometimes-ingenious ways of crossing the border. Some have taken to posing as senior citizens on bus trips to buy cheap Canadian prescription drugs. After catching a half-dozen young vegans disguised in powdered wigs, Canadian immigration authorities began stopping buses and quizzing the supposed senior-citizen passengers.

"If they can't identify the accordion player on *The Lawrence Welk Show*, we get suspicious about their age," an official said. Canadian citizens have complained that the illegal immigrants are creating an organic-broccoli shortage and renting all the good Susan Sarandon movies.

"I feel sorry for American liberals, but the Canadian economy just can't support them," an Ottawa resident said. "How many art-history majors does one country need?"

In an effort to ease tensions between the United States and Canada, Vice President Dick Cheney met with the Canadian ambassador and pledged that the administration would take steps to reassure liberals, a source close to Cheney said.

"We're going to have some Peter, Paul & Mary concerts. And we might put some endangered species on postage stamps. The president is determined to reach out."

So, you may be asking at this point, how did it get this way? Why is there such a division between liberals and conservatives? The answer is surprisingly simple. You see, the division of the human family into two distinct political groups began some 12,000 years ago. At that time humans existed as members of small bands of nomadic hunter gatherers who lived on deer in the mountains in the summer, and went to the beach and live on fish and lobster in winter.

The two most important events in all of history were the invention of beer and the invention of the wheel. The wheel was invented to get man to the beer. This was the foundation of modern civilization, and was the catalyst for splitting humanity into two distinct subgroups.

Once beer was discovered it required grain, and that was the beginning of agriculture. Neither the glass bottle nor aluminum can was invented yet, so while our early human ancestors were sitting around waiting for them to be invented, they just stayed close to the brewery. That's how villages were formed.

Some men spent their days tracking and killing animals to BBQ at night while they were drinking beer. This was the beginning of what is known as the Conservative Movement. Other men who were weaker and less skilled at hunting, learned to live off the conservatives by showing up for the nightly BBQ and doing the sewing, fetching and hair dressing. This was the beginning of the Liberal Movement. Some of these liberal men eventually evolved into women, and the rest became known as "girliemen."

Some noteworthy liberal achievements include the domestication of cats, the trade union, the invention of group therapy and hugs, and the concept of Democratic voting to decide how to divide the meat and beer the conservatives provided. Over time conservatives came to be symbolized by the largest, most powerful land animal on earth, the elephant, while liberals are symbolized by the jackass.

Modern liberals like imported beer (with lime), but most prefer white wine or imported bottled water. They eat raw fish, but like their beef well done. Sushi, tofu, and French food are standard liberal fare. Most social workers, personal injury attorneys, journalists, dreamers in Hollywood and group therapists are liberals. Liberals invented the designated hitter rule in baseball, because it wasn't "fair" to make the pitcher also bat.

Conservatives drink domestic beer. The men eat red meat and still provide for their women. They are big-game hunters, rodeo cowboys, lumberjacks, construction workers, medical doctors, police officers, corporate executives, soldiers, athletes, and generally anyone who works productively outside government. Conservatives who own companies hire others who want to work for a living.

Liberals produce little or nothing. They like to "govern" the producers, and decide what to do with the production. Liberals believe Europeans are more enlightened than Americans. That is why most of them remained in Europe when conservatives were coming to America. They crept in later after the Wild West was tamed, and created a business of trying to get MORE for nothing.

And you thought history was boring! Now that the history lesson is over, let's move on to a humorous examination of the Democrat Party and some prominent members of their party.

TABLE OF CONTENTS

DUMMYCRATS

DNC CHAIRMAN
(which one is unimportant)

A tourist walks into a curio shop in San Francisco. Looking around at everything, he notices a very lifelike life-sized bronze statue of a rat. It has no price tag, but is so striking that he decides he must have it. He takes it to the owner and asks, "How much for the bronze rat?"

The owner replies, "$12 for the rat, and $100 for the story."

The tourist gives the man $12 and says, "I'll just take the rat, you can keep the story."

As he walks down the street carrying his bronze rat, he notices that a few real rats have crawled out of the alleys and sewers and begun following him down the street. This is disconcerting, and he begins walking faster, but within a couple of blocks the herd of rats behind him has grown to hundreds, and they begin squealing. He begins to trot toward the Bay, and notices that the rats now number in the MILLIONS, and are squealing and coming toward him faster and faster.

Terrified, he runs to the edge of the bay and throws the bronze rat as far out into the water as he can. Amazingly, the millions of rats all jump into the bay after it, and are all drowned. Regaining his composure, the man walks back to the curio shop.

"Ah ha," says the owner, "I see you have come back for the story."

"No," says the man, "I came back to see if you have a bronze Democrat!"

* * * * *

Dear Abby,

I am a crack dealer in Beaumont, Texas who has recently been diagnosed as a carrier of the HIV virus. My parents live in a trailer park in Fort Worth and one of my sisters, who lives in Pflugerville, is married to a transvestite.

My father and mother have recently been arrested for growing and selling marijuana. They are financially dependent on my other two sisters, who are prostitutes in Dallas. I have two brothers, one of whom is currently serving a non-parole life sentence at Huntsville for the murder of a teenage boy in 1994. My other brother is currently in jail awaiting charges of sexual misconduct with his three children.

I recently became engaged to marry a former prostitute from Longview who is still a part time "working girl." All things considered, my problem is this. I love my fiancé and look forward to bringing her into the family, and I certainly want to be totally open and honest with her.

Here's the problem. Should I tell her about my cousin, the Democrat?

Signed,
Worried About My Reputation

* * * * *

"Last year, the vice president launched a new effort to help make communities more liberal." - *Bill Clinton, attempting to praise Al Gore during his 2000 State of the Union Speech. He meant to say "more livable," and made the same slip-up in a subsequent sentence, drawing uproarious laughter from Republicans. Talk about a Freudain slip!*

* * * * *

"John Edwards is a seasoned trial lawyer. You think a lawyer would make a good president? You know I look at it this way, if we're going to consistently have liars in the White House, why not get a professional?" - Jay Leno

* * * * *

"Howard Dean, once the Democratic front runner, said if he does not win the Wisconsin primary on February 17th he will drop out of the race. Dean made the announcement by telling a group of supporters 'We will *not* go to Oklahoma, or Indiana, or Kansas. We will *not* go to Texas, or Kentucky, or Pennsylvania, or New York IIIIIIIEIEI!!!'" - Jimmy Fallon, Saturday Night Live

* * * * *

"Under everyone's seat in the House of Representatives last night, there was a foil package containing a hood in case there was a chemical and biological attack. One embarrassing moment last night. Senator Robert Byrd opened the hood and said, 'Shouldn't there be a white robe in here too?'"
- Jay Leno

"Al Sharpton said the Democratic Party has to stop treating blacks as their mistresses. Sharpton then explained a mistress is where they take you out to have fun, but they don't take you home. Was it really necessary to explain what a mistress is to Democrats?" - Jay Leno

"Today, on the coldest day in over fifty years, Al Gore gave a speech attacking President Bush on global warming. Good timing Al. First he grew a beard right before the terrorist attacks - that was smart. Now he is talking about global warming in the middle of winter. What's next - cutting the ribbon at the Michael Jackson Daycare Center?"
- Jay Leno

"In (Pete Rose's new book) he admits that he used to date cocktail waitresses, groupies and strippers. I don't know if that will keep him out of the Hall of Fame, but he is now the leading candidate for the Democratic nomination." - Jay Leno

* * * * *

"Isn't spring in New York fantastic? The great thing about spring is that it comes once a year... just like a Kennedy trial." - David Letterman

* * * * *

"Democratic leader Tom Daschle has been whining all over TV, saying that Rush Limbaugh and other talk show hosts have been inciting violence against Democrats. Which is illegal you know, attacking an endangered species." - Jay Leno

* * * * *

"The Democrats have selected Boston, Massachusetts as the sight of the 2004 Democratic Convention. The convention will be held in September. This way the Red Sox and the Democrats can face mathematical elimination together." - Jay Leno

* * * * *

"In Ohio, some people will be going to the polls to re-elect disgraced Democratic Congressman James Trafficant, even though he's currently in prison. That actually makes sense. I guess if he's already in jail, it saves a step." - Jay Leno

* * * * *

"Here's a great story. Incoming Senate Majority Leader Bill Frist, who is a heart surgeon, was driving while on vacation in Florida, saw an SUV overturned on the highway, stopped, got out of the car, jumped over and helped the victims until the paramedics arrived. But he was not the only senator who stopped at the accident. Trial lawyer John Edwards stopped and chased the ambulance all the way to the hospital." - Jay Leno

* * * * *

"Janet Reno lost the Democratic primary in Florida. When asked about it, Reno said, 'I feel like I've been kicked in the nuts.'" - Conan O'Brien

* * * * *

"The Democrats said today that if they were in power they could get Israel to pull out of Palestine. Oh shut up. They couldn't even get Bill to pull out of Monica." - Jay Leno

* * * * *

Q: Who was the first Democrat?
A: Christopher Columbus. He left not knowing where he was going, got there not knowing where he was, left not knowing where he'd been and did it all on borrowed money.

* * * * *

A teacher in a small Vermont town asked her class how many of them were Democrats. Not really knowing what a Democrat was, but wanting to be liked by the teacher, all of the kids raise their hands except one boy. The teacher asked Johnny why he has decided to be different.

"Because I'm not a Democrat." Johnny said.

"Why not?" the teacher asked.

Johnny said, "I'm a Republican."

The teacher then asked why he was Republican.

The boy said, "Well, my mom's a Republican, and my dad's a Republican, so I'm a Republican!"

The teacher was kind of angry, because after all this was Vermont, so she then asked, "What if your mom was a moron, and your dad was an idiot? What that would make you?"

Johnny said, "*That* would make me a Democrat!"

Question: How do you tell the difference between Democrats and Republicans?
Answer: Pose the following question:

You're walking down a deserted street with your wife and two small children. Suddenly, a dangerous looking man with a huge knife comes around the corner, locks eyes with you, screams obscenities, raises the knife, and charges. You are carrying a Glock .40, and you are an expert shot. You have mere seconds before he reaches you and your family.

What would *you* do?

Democrat's Answer:

Well, that's not enough information to answer the question! Does the man look poor or oppressed? Have I ever done anything to him that would inspire him to attack? Could we run away? What does my wife think? What about the kids? Could I possibly swing the gun like a club and knock the knife out of his hand? What does the law say about this situation? Does the Glock have appropriate safety built into it? Why am I carrying a loaded gun anyway, and what kind of message does this send to society and to my children? Is it possible he'd be happy with killing just me? Does he definitely want to kill me, or would he be content just to wound me? If I were to grab his knees and hold on, could my family get away while he was stabbing me? Should I call 9-1-1? Why is this street so deserted? We need to raise taxes, have a paint and weed day and make this a happier, healthier street that would discourage such behavior. This is so confusing! I need to debate this with some friends for a few days and try to come to a consensus.

Republican's Answer: BANG!

* * * * *

"The Ohio Democratic Party has named raunchy former talk show host Jerry Springer as a delegate to the Democrat National Convention in Boston, the Associated Press reports. The party also named Springer 'Democrat of the Year.' Imagine how humiliating this was to the runner-up!" - James Taranto

* * * * *

Nancy Pelosi was out walking one morning and noticed Little Hannah sitting on the corner with a box. Curious, Pelosi went over to her and said, "What's in the box, kid?"

Little Hannah said, "Kittens, they're brand new kittens."

Pelosi laughed and said, "What kind of kittens are they?"

"Democrats," replied Little Hannah.

"Oh that's cute," she said and went on her way.

A few days later Pelosi was walking with her buddy Harry Reid and spied Little Hannah with her box of kitten just ahead. She said to Harry, "You gotta check this out," and they both walked over to where the little girl was sitting.

Pelosi said, "Look in the box Harry, isn't that cute? Look at those little kittens. Hey kid, tell my friend Harry what kind of kittens they are."

Little Hannah replied, "They're Republicans."

"Whoa!" Pelosi said, "when I came by here the other day you said they were Democrats. What's up with that?"

"Well," Little Hannah explained, "their eyes are *open* now."

* * * * *

THE ANT AND THE GRASSHOPPER

OLD VERSION:

The ant works hard in the withering heat all summer long, building his house and laying up supplies for the winter.

The grasshopper thinks he's a fool and laughs and dances and plays the summer away. Come winter, the ant is warm and well fed. The grasshopper has no food or shelter, so he dies out in the cold.

MORAL OF THE STORY: Be responsible for yourself!

MODERN VERSION:

The ant works hard in the withering heat all summer long, building his house and laying up supplies for the winter.

The grasshopper thinks he's a fool and laughs and dances and plays the summer away.

Come winter, the shivering grasshopper calls a press conference and demands to know why the ant should be allowed to be warm and well fed while others are cold and starving.

CNN, CBS, NBC, and ABC show up to provide pictures of the shivering grasshopper next to a video of the ant in his comfortable home with a table filled with food. America is stunned by the sharp contrast. How can this be, that in a country of such wealth, this poor grasshopper is allowed to suffer so?

Kermit the Frog appears on *Oprah* with the grasshopper, and everybody cries when they sing, *It's Not Easy Being Green.*

Jesse Jackson stages a demonstration in front of the ant's house where the news stations film the group singing, *We Shall Overcome.* Jesse then has the group kneel down to pray to God for the grasshopper's sake.

Nancy Pelosi and Harry Reid exclaim in an interview with Chris Matthews that the ant has gotten rich off the back of the grasshopper, and both call for an immediate tax hike on the ant to make him pay his "fair share."

Finally, the EEOC drafts the "Economic Equity and Anti-Grasshopper Act," retroactive to the beginning of the summer. The ant is fined for failing to hire a proportionate number of green bugs and, having nothing left with which to pay his retroactive taxes, his home is confiscated by the government.

John Edwards gets his law firm to represent the grasshopper in a defamation suit against the ant, and the case is tried before a panel of federal judges that Barack Obama appointed from a list of single-parent welfare recipients.

The ant loses the case.

The story ends as we see the grasshopper finishing up the last bits of the ant's food while the government house he is in, which just happens to be the ant's old house, crumbles around him because he doesn't maintain it. The ant has disappeared in the snow.

The grasshopper is later found dead in a drug related incident and the house, now abandoned, is taken over by a gang of spiders who terrorize the once peaceful neighborhood.

MORAL OF THE STORY: Vote Republican!

* * * * *

Imagine you are a rancher living in California, and have a cow and a bull. The bull is depressed. It has spent its life living a lie, so it goes away for two weeks and comes back after a taxpayer-paid sex-change operation. You now have two cows. One makes milk, and the other doesn't. You try to sell the transgender cow, and its lawyer sues you for discrimination. You lose in court, and sell the milk-generating cow to pay the damages.

You now have one rich, transgender, non-milk-producing cow, so you change your business to beef. PETA pickets your farm, Jesse Jackson makes a speech in your driveway and La Raza threatens you because you have no Mexican cows. Barack Obama calls for higher farm taxes to help "working cows." Nancy Pelosi calls for the nationalization of 1/7 of your farm "for the children," but Jerry Brown had already signed a law giving your farm to Mexico.

The *L.A. Times* quotes five anonymous cows who claim you groped their teats, you declare bankruptcy and shut down all operations, the cow starves to death, and the *L.A. Times'* analysis shows your business failure is all George W. Bush's fault.

* * * * *

A college student who considered herself a liberal came home during spring break to visit her father, who was a staunch conservative. After some small talk he asked how she was doing in school, and the daughter replied her grade point average was a perfect 4.0. She added that it wasn't easy, because maintaining that level of achievement required her to study long hours and have virtually no social life.

The father then inquired about his daughter's best friend Nancy, who was also attending the same university. She answered that her friend was barely able to maintain a 2.0 GPA, mainly because she dated a lot, went to parties and rarely studied.

Upon hearing that the father asked if it was possible to have the school take one point from the daughter's average and transfer it to her friend so that they would have equal 3.0 GPAs.

The daughter, shocked that her dad would suggest such a thing, exclaimed, "That wouldn't be fair! I earned my grades by working hard, while Nancy is barely making an effort!"

The father let the lesson sink in for a moment, and quietly replied, "Welcome to the Republican Party."

* * * * *

Barack Obama, Nancy Pelosi and Harry Reid were flying on Air Force One. Obama looked at Pelosi, chuckled and said, "You know, I could throw a one hundred dollar bill out the window right now and make somebody down on the ground very happy."

Pelosi shrugged her shoulders and said, "Well, I could make change and throw ten dollar bills out the window and make *ten* people very happy."

Reid said, "Even better, I could throw one hundred one dollar bills out the window and make a *hundred* people happy."

The Air Force Colonel flying the aircraft rolled his eyes, looked at the three of them and said to his co-pilot, "You know, we could throw all of *them* out the window and make *everybody* happy!"

* * * * *

A woman in a hot air balloon realized she was lost, so she lowered her altitude and spotted a man in a boat below. She shouted to him, "Excuse me, can you help me? I promised a friend I would meet him an hour ago, but I don't know where I am."

The man consulted his portable GPS and replied, "You're in a hot air balloon, approximately thirty feet above a ground elevation of 2346 feet above sea level. You are at 31 degrees, 14.97 minutes north latitude and 100 degrees, 49.09 minutes west longitude."

She rolled her eyes and said in exasperation, "You must be a Republican."

"I am," replied the man. "How did you know?"

"Well," answered the balloonist, "everything you told me is technically correct, but I have no idea what to do with your information, and I'm still lost. Frankly, you've not been much help to me."

The man smiled and responded, "Well then, *you* must be a Democrat."

"I am," replied the balloonist. "How did you know?"

"Well," said the man, "you don't know where you are or where you're going. You've risen to where you are due to a large quantity of hot air. You made a promise that you have no idea how to keep, and you expect me to solve your problem for you. And finally, you're in exactly the same position you were in before we met but yet, somehow, it's now *my* fault!"

* * * * *

I was traveling between Phoenix and Chicago the other day and was south of Kansas City when a tire blew out. Checking my spare, I found that it too was flat. My only option was to flag down a passing motorist and get a ride to the next town.

The first vehicle to stop was an old man in a van. He yelled out the window, "Need a lift?"

"Yes, I sure do," I replied.

"You a Democrat or Republican?" asked the old man.

"Republican," I replied.

"Well, you can just go to Hell," yelled the old man as he sped off.

Another guy stopped, rolled down the window, and asked me the same question. Again, I gave the same answer, "Republican."

The driver gave me the finger and drove off.

I thought it over and decided that maybe I should change my strategy, since this area seemed to be overly political and there appeared to be few Republicans.

The next car to stop was a red convertible driven by a beautiful blonde. She smiled seductively and asked if I was a Democrat or Republican.

"Democrat!" I shouted.

"Hop in!" replied the blonde.

As we drove down the road I couldn't help but stare at this gorgeous woman in the seat next to me, with the wind blowing through her hair, perfect breasts, and a short skirt that continued to ride higher and higher up her thighs.

Finally I yelled, "Please stop the car!"

She immediately slammed on the brakes, and as soon as the car stopped I jumped out.

"What's the matter?" she asked."

I can't take it anymore," I replied. "I've only been a Democrat for five minutes, and I *already* want to screw somebody!"

* * * * *

Once upon a time, a Sultan was blessed with the birth of a son after years of hoping. The boy immediately became the apple of his father's eye.

Just before his son's sixth birthday the Sultan said to him, "Son, I love you very much. Your birthday is coming soon. What would you like?"

His son replied, "Daddy, I would like to have my own airplane."

So his father bought him American Airlines.

Just before his son's seventh birthday the Sultan said, "Son, you are my pride and joy. Ask what you want for your birthday. Whatever it is, it's yours."

His son replied, "Daddy, I would like a boat."

So his father bought him Princess Cruise Lines.

Just before his son's eighth birthday the Sultan said, "Son, you bring so much happiness into my life. Anything you want, I shall get for you."

His son replied, "Daddy, I would like to be able to watch cartoons."

So his father bought him Disney Studios, which made the son very happy.

Just before his son's ninth birthday the Sultan said, "Son, you are my life. Your birthday is coming soon. Ask what you wish. I will get it for you."

His son, who had grown to love Disney, replied, "Daddy, I would like a Mickey Mouse outfit."

And so his father bought him the Democratic Party.

* * * * *

A Republican in a wheelchair entered a restaurant one afternoon and asked the waitress for a cup of coffee. The Republican looked across the restaurant and asked, "Is that Jesus sitting over there?"

The waitress nodded and said "Yes, it is," so the Republican requested that she give Jesus a cup of coffee on him.

The next patron to come in was a Libertarian with a hunched back. He shuffled over to a booth, painfully sat down, and asked the waitress for a cup of hot tea. He also glanced across the restaurant and asked, "Is that Jesus over there?" The waitress nodded, so the Libertarian asked her to give Jesus a cup of hot tea, "My treat."

The third patron to come into the restaurant was a Democrat on crutches. He hobbled over to a booth, sat down and hollered, "Hey there, honey! How's about getting me a cold glass of Miller Light!" He too looked across the restaurant and asked, "Is that

God's boy over there?" The waitress once more nodded, so the Democrat directed her to give Jesus a cold glass of beer. "On my bill," he said.

As Jesus got up to leave he passed by the Republican, touched him and said, "For your kindness, you are healed." The Republican felt the strength come back into his legs, got up, and danced a jig out the door.

Jesus then passed by the Libertarian, touched him and said, "For your kindness, you are healed." The Libertarian felt his back straightening up, and he raised his hands, praised the Lord and did a series of back flips out the door.

Then Jesus walked towards the Democrat. The Democrat jumped up and yelled, "Don't you dare touch me! I'm collecting disability!"

* * * * *

AMERICAN HISTORY LESSON

➤ Abraham Lincoln was elected to Congress in 1846, and John F. Kennedy was elected to Congress in 1946.

➤ Abraham Lincoln was elected President in 1860, and John F. Kennedy was elected President in 1960.

➤ Lincoln's secretary was named Kennedy, and Kennedy's secretary was named Lincoln.

➢ The names Lincoln and Kennedy each contain seven letters.
➢ Both men were concerned with civil rights.
➢ Both of their wives lost children while living in the White House.
➢ Both Presidents were shot on a Friday.
➢ Both Presidents were shot in the head.
➢ Both were succeeded by Southerners named Johnson.
➢ Andrew Johnson, who succeeded Lincoln, was born in 1808. Lyndon Johnson, who succeeded Kennedy, was born in 1908.
➢ John Wilkes Booth, who assassinated Lincoln, was born in 1839. Lee Harvey Oswald, who assassinated Kennedy, was born in 1939.
➢ Both assassins were known by their three names.
➢ Both names are composed of fifteen letters.
➢ Lincoln was shot while at a theater named Ford. Kennedy was shot in a car called Lincoln, made by Ford.
➢ Booth ran from the theater and was caught in a warehouse. Oswald ran from a warehouse and was caught in a theater.
➢ Both Booth and Oswald were assassinated before their trials.
➢ And here's the kicker… a week before Lincoln was shot, he was in Monroe, Maryland. A week before Kennedy was shot, he was in Marilyn Monroe.

OSAMA-BAMA

Barack Obama was tossing restlessly in his bed, and awakened to see George Washington standing in the bedroom. He asked, "George, what is the best thing I can do to help the country?"

"Set an honest and honorable example, like I did," advised Washington before fading away.

The next night Obama saw the ghost of Thomas Jefferson, and called out, "Tom, what is the best thing I can do to help the country?"

"Respect the Constitution, like I did," replied Jefferson as he faded away.

The next night Obama still can't sleep, and found the ghost of F.D.R. in the room. He whispered, "Franklin, what is the best thing I can do to help the country?"

"Help the people, just like I did," F.D.R. replied before he disappeared.

The next night Obama is still too restless to sleep, and across the room he saw the ghost of Abraham Lincoln. He asked, "Abe, what is the best thing I can do to help the country?"

Abe replied, "Go see a play…"

* * * * *

President Obama decided to do one of his public addresses against the backdrop of an American farm, but the ceremony couldn't get started because of all the flies buzzing around his head.

Obama demanded to know why the flies wouldn't leave, so the farmer explained to him, "Well, those are called circle flies. They always circle around the back end of horses."

Obama angrily replied, "Hey, are you saying that I'm a horse's ass?"

The farmer answered, "No Sir, Mister President. I would never call someone a horse's ass. It's hard to fool them flies, though!"

* * * * *

A man died and went to heaven, and as he stood in front of St. Peter at the Pearly Gates he saw a huge wall of clocks behind him and asked, "What are all those clocks?"

St. Peter smiled and answered, "Those are Lie-Clocks. Everyone on earth has a Lie-Clock. Every time you lie, the hands on your clock will move."

"Oh," said the man. "Whose clock is that?"

"That's Mother Teresa's. The hands have never moved, indicating that she never told a lie."

"Incredible," said the man. "And what about that one?"

St. Peter responded, "That's Abraham Lincoln's clock. The hands have moved twice, telling us that Abe told only two lies in his entire life."

"Where's Barack Obama's clock?" asked the man.

"It's in Jesus' office. He's using it as a ceiling fan."

In 2011 Groundhog Day and Obama's State of the Union address occurred on the same date. One event involves a meaningless ritual in which we look to a creature of little intelligence for prognostication, while the other involves a groundhog.

* * * * *

Obama has a new plan to save American jobs. He and Michelle are going to personally keep the vacation planners busy.

* * * * *

It's a 'recession' when your neighbor loses his job, it's a 'depression' when you lose your job, and it's a 'recovery' when Barack Obama loses his job.

* * * * *

The Obama economy utilizes a system of carefully monitored checks and balances. He writes the checks, we pay the balances.

* * * * *

"It's so bad for Obama that now *Democrats* want to see his birth certificate!" - Jay Leno

* * * * *

"Obama said he will attend the Nobel Peace Prize ceremony in Oslo if he's not too busy with the two wars he's conducting." - Bill Maher

* * * * *

The liberals are asking us to give Obama time. We agree... and think 25 to life would be appropriate.

* * * * *

Do you remember the Reagan era, when Ronald Reagan was President, and Bob Hope and Johnny Cash were still with us? Well, now we have the Obama era, along with no hope, and no cash.

* * * * *

Q. Why did Obama cross the road?
A. Actually, Obama *promised* to cross the road, but then he didn't.

* * * * *

Q. What did Obama and Osama have in common?
A. They both had friends who bombed the Pentagon.

* * * * *

"How many watched the Obama speech on Tuesday night? If you didn't see it, I'll give you the short version. We're completely broke and deeply in debt, but we're going to do a bank rescue, universal healthcare, give everybody a college education, have a bigger war in Afghanistan, cut the deficit in half, and cure cancer." - Bill Maher

* * * * *

37

"Police in Texas arrested a man who was using the alias 'Barack Obama' while trying to steal money from several ATMs. They could tell something was up when a guy named Barack Obama was trying to *take* money from banks instead of *giving* it to them." - Jimmy Fallon

* * * * *

"We are a year into Obama's first term in office and unemployment is higher, the national debt is higher and there are more soldiers serving in Afghanistan. When asked about it, Obama was like, "Well, technically that *is* change.' - Jimmy Fallon

* * * * *

"That's pretty amazing, Obama winning the Nobel Peace Prize. Ironically, his biggest accomplishment as president so far is: winning the Nobel Peace Prize." - Jay Leno

* * * * *

"The President held a press conference tonight in prime time. All of the major networks carried it, except Fox. They ran the show *Lie to Me* instead.
- Jimmy Kimmel

* * * * *

"Big day in Detroit. You may have heard about this. The Obama Administration asked General Motors CEO Rick Wagoner to step down, and he agreed, which is good news for Obama. You know, the last time he tried to get someone to quit, it took months. And even then, he had to promise her a job as Secretary of State." - Jay Leno

* * * * *

"Did you see this on *60 Minutes* last night? Michelle Obama is planting a vegetable garden on the White House lawn. You *know* the economy's bad when the Obamas are afraid of running out of food!" - Jimmy Fallon

* * * * *

"I've now been in 57 states - I think one left to go."
- Barack Obama, at a campaign event in Beaverton, Oregon (imagine if Bush had said that!)

* * * * *

"Barack Obama said yesterday that the economy was 'going to get worse before it gets better.' See, that's when you know the campaign is really over. Remember before the election? The audacity of hope!... Yes, we can!... Change we can believe in!... Now it's 'We're all screwed.'" - Jay Leno

* * * * *

"The economy is in bad shape. In fact, the economy is so bad, President Barack Obama's new slogan is 'Spare Change You Can Believe In.'" - Jay Leno

* * * * *

"Barack Obama plans to issue an executive order on his first full day in office, directing the closing of Guantanamo Bay. He said he needs the money for new prisons to hold Democratic mayors and governors." - Jay Leno

* * * * *

"The reforms we seek would bring greater competition, choice, savings and inefficiencies to our health care system." - Barack Obama making a Freudian slip, in remarks after a health care roundtable with physicians, nurses and health care providers, Washington, D.C., July 20, 2009

* * * * *

"The White House said that President Obama will not focus on full-time campaigning for a long time. Yeah, he wants to wait a year or two before he gets serious about it - just like he did with being president." - Jimmy Fallon

* * * * *

Q: What's the difference between Obama's cabinet and a penitentiary?
A: One is filled with tax evaders, blackmailers and threats to society. The other is for housing prisoners.

* * * * *

"UPS and FedEx are doing just fine, right? It's the Post Office that's always having problems."
- Barack Obama, attempting to make the case for government run health care, while simultaneously undercutting his own argument, Portsmouth, N.H., Aug. 11, 2009

* * * * *

"It was also interesting to see that political interaction in Europe is not that different from the United States Senate. There's a lot of - I don't know what the term is in Austrian, wheeling and dealing."
- Barack Obama, confusing German for "'Austrian,'" a language which does not exist, Strasbourg, France, April 6, 2009

* * * * *

"In case you missed it, this week there was a tragedy in Kansas. Ten thousand people died - an entire town destroyed." - Barack Obama, on a Kansas tornado that killed a total of 12 people

* * * * *

Q. Why doesn't Obama pray?
A. It's impossible to read the teleprompter with your eyes closed.

* * * * *

"What I was suggesting - you're absolutely right that John McCain has not talked about my Muslim faith..." - Barack Obama, in an interview with ABC's George Stephanopoulos, who jumped in to correct Obama by saying "your *Christian* faith," which Obama quickly clarified

* * * * *

Q. Why did Jimmy Carter vote for Barack Obama?
A. Because Jimmy didn't want to be the worst President in history anymore.

* * * * *

America needs Obama-care like Nancy Pelosi needs a Halloween mask.

* * * * *

Q: Have you heard about McDonalds' new Obama Value Meal?
A: Order anything you like, and the guy behind you in line has to pay for it.

* * * * *

Q: What does Barack Obama call lunch with a convicted felon?
A: A fund raiser.

* * * * *

Q: If Nancy Pelosi and Obama were on a boat in the middle of the ocean and it started to sink, who would be saved?
A: America!

* * * * *

Q: What's the difference between Obama and his dog, Bo?
A: Bo has papers.

* * * * *

Q: What was the most positive result of the "Cash for Clunkers" program?
A: It took 95% of the Obama bumper stickers off the road.

* * * * *

"Barack Obama gave a big speech on race, and there was one heckler in the audience who kept screaming crazy stuff the whole time. Turns out it was his pastor." - Jay Leno

* * * * *

"President Obama is going to seek reelection. His slogan this time? 'Change you can believe in. This time I promise. Really.'" - Jay Leno

* * * * *

"President Obama announced his re-election campaign, though it's not really a surprise. He did all the things that make it official: He filed the paperwork, redesigned his website, and printed another fake birth certificate." - Craig Ferguson

* * * * *

"I want to say happy birthday today to Barack Obama. The president just turned 48 years old - if he was ever really born, that is. Obama's birthday is a reminder of why health care is so important. As you probably know, due to a lack of health care coverage, Obama's mother was turned away from a number of hospitals and was ultimately forced to give birth in a manger." - Jimmy Fallon

* * * * *

"The situation is deteriorating in Libya and Japan and the stock market is collapsing worldwide. President Obama finally took decisive action. He named Duke, Kansas, Ohio State and Pittsburgh as his Final Four." - Jay Leno

* * * * *

Obama motto: "A penny saved is a penny taxed."

* * * * *

"I think when you spread the wealth around, it's good for everybody." - Barack Obama, defending his tax plan to "Joe the Plumber," who argued that Obama's policy hurts small-business owners like himself, Toledo, Ohio, Oct. 12, 2008

* * * * *

"President Obama said he was always getting in trouble when he was in middle school. In fact, Obama said he talked so much during class, the teacher had to take away his teleprompter." - Jimmy Fallon

* * * * *

"President Barack Obama told his Cabinet yesterday to insure that every taxpayer dollar is spent wisely. But there was one embarrassing moment when he had to explain to the Cabinet what a taxpayer was." - Jay Leno

* * * * *

"So Obama gave the Queen an iPod. I remember when British Prime Minister Gordon Brown was here, the Obamas gave him a DVD box set. So, it looks like they're saving the big gift, the Nintendo, for the Pope." - Jay Leno

* * * * *

"The Middle East is obviously an issue that has plagued the region for centuries." - Barack Obama, Jan. 28, 2010

* * * * *

"President Obama just held his first monthly bipartisan meeting and said that working together on jobs would be a good place to start. You know where else would have been a good place to start? A year ago!" - Jimmy Fallon

* * * * *

"In a surprise decision, President Obama won the 2009 Nobel Peace Prize on Friday. In other premature awards this week: high school football player Billy Reynolds has been named this year's Heisman Trophy winner; fifth grader Amber Collins has been named Miss America; and nine-year-old Dylan Holt has been named *People's* 'Sexiest Man Alive.'" - Seth Meyers

* * * * *

"One such translator was an American of Haitian descent, representative of the extraordinary work that our men and women in uniform do all around the world - Navy Corpse-Man Christian Brossard."
- Barack Obama, mispronouncing "Corpsman" (the "ps" is silent) during a speech at the National Prayer Breakfast, Washington, D.C., Feb. 5, 2010 (the Corpsman's name is also Christopher, not Christian)

* * * * *

46

"No, no. I have been practicing... I bowled a 129. It's like... it was like the Special Olympics, or something." - Barack Obama, making an off-hand joke during an appearance on The Tonight Show, March 19, 2009 (Obama later called the head of the Special Olympics to apologize)

* * * * *

"Now, what we are doing, I want to be clear, we are not trying to push financial reform because we begrudge success that's fairly earned. I mean, I do think at a certain point you've made enough money." - Barack Obama, on Wall Street reform, Quincy, Ill., April 29, 2010

* * * * *

President Obama was being criticized because his inaugural celebrations cost the taxpayers over $400 million. When asked about it Obama explained Ted Kennedy had attended, and there was an open bar.

* * * * *

Barack Obama walked into a bar with a frog on his head, sat down and asked for a drink.

The bartender saw the frog on his head and said, "What in the hell happened to you?"

The frog replied, "Well, it all started with a wart on my ass..."

* * * * *

Working people frequently ask retired people what they do to make their days interesting. Well, for example, the other day I went downtown and into a shop. I was only there for about five minutes, and when I came out there was a cop writing out a parking ticket.

I said to him, "Come on man, how about giving a retired person a break"? He ignored me and continued writing the ticket.

I called him a "Nazi." He glared at me and wrote another ticket for having worn tires. So I called him a "doughnut eating Gestapo."

He finished the second ticket and put it on the windshield with the first. Then he wrote a third ticket. This went on for about twenty minutes. The more I abused him, the more tickets he wrote.

Personally, I didn't care. I had come downtown on the bus, and the car that he was putting the tickets on had a bumper sticker that said, "Obama in '08." I try to have a little fun each day now that I'm retired. It's important to my health.

* * * * *

Under an Obama presidency the IRS will be more diligent about detecting red flags, like any leftover money you may have in your bank account after you pay your taxes.

* * * * *

Q. What's an example of irony?
A. Bruce Springsteen sang *Born in the USA* at Barack Obama's inauguration.

* * * * *

Q. What is the difference between President Obama and Karl Marx?
A. If you can figure that one out, please let us know.

* * * * *

President Obama has just announced that he has a new plan to simplify the tax code. From now on only Republicans will have to have to pay taxes.

* * * * *

Like any experienced Chicago politician, Obama would go the cemetery to register voters. One night he came across a grave so old and worn that he couldn't make out the name on the tombstone. The staffer holding the flashlight got impatient and suggested they just move on to the next plot. Obama angrily exclaimed, "This person has a much right to vote as the guy in the *next* grave!"

* * * * *

TOP TEN INDICATORS YOUR EMPLOYER HAS CHANGED TO OBAMACARE

10. Your annual breast exam is done at Hooters.

9. Directions to your doctor's office include "Take a left when you enter the trailer park."

8. The tongue depressors taste faintly like a Fudgesicle.

7. The only proctologist in the plan is "Gus" from Roto-Rooter.

6. The only item listed under Preventive Care Coverage is "An apple a day..."

5. Your primary care physician is wearing the coveralls you gave to Goodwill last month.

4. Where it says, "The patient is responsible for 200% of out-of-network charges," it's not a typographical error.

3. The only expense that is 100% covered is "embalming."

2. Your Prozac comes in different colors with little M's on them.

1. You ask for Viagra and they give you a Popsicle stick and some duct tape.

BIN-BIDEN

A priest was being honored at his retirement dinner after 25 years in the parish. A leading local politician and member of the congregation was chosen to make the presentation and give a little speech at the dinner, but he was delayed so the priest decided to say a few words of his own while they waited.

"I got my first impression of the parish from the first confession I heard here. I thought I had been assigned to a terrible place. The very first person who entered my confessional told me he had stolen a television set, and when stopped by the police had almost murdered the officer. He had stolen money from his parents, embezzled from his place of business, had an affair with his boss's wife, taken illegal drugs, and gave VD to his sister.

I was appalled... but as the days went on I knew that my people were not all like that, and I had indeed come to a fine parish full good and loving people."

Just as the priest finished his talk, Joe Biden arrived full of apologies for being late. He immediately began to make the presentation and give his talk. "I'll never forget the first day our parish priest arrived," said Biden. "In fact, I had the honor of being the first one to go to him in confession..."

* * * * *

The Obama administration wants a new simplified tax form that will be idiot proof. They'll test it out on Joe Biden.

* * * * *

When they moved into the White House, Barack Obama got a dog for his daughters. And he was very clear, he was very strict - he said, "You're gonna have to feed it, you're gonna have to give it water, and you're gonna have to clean up after it, do you understand that?" And Joe Biden said, "Yeah..." - Jay Leno

* * * * *

Joe Biden was trying to sell his clunker that had already been driven 310,000 miles, but he was having a mighty hard time with it. Barack Obama offered to help him out and turned the car odometer back to just 10,000 miles. The President asked Biden a few days later whether he had been able to sell the clunker. "Why would I want to sell it?" asked Biden. "There's only 10,000 miles on it!"

* * * * *

"Vice President Joe Biden said there has been no 'substantive damage' to the United States by Julian Assange in the whole WikiLeaks scandal. He says it has been embarrassing, but you can't prosecute people for embarrassing the United States. And he's right - if that were true, Joe Biden would be serving life in prison!" – Jay Leno

* * * * *

"The Obamas have chosen a new White House dog. It is a Portuguese water dog named Bo. Very cute dog. Their first choice was a wheaten terrier, but it was arrested for tax evasion. Bo arrived just in time, because Sasha and Malia were getting tired of throwing Frisbees at Joe Biden." - Jimmy Fallon

* * * * *

"Sir Paul McCartney played at the White House last night. He dedicated the Beatles song *Michelle* to the First Lady. Isn't that lovely? And then for Joe Biden, he played *Fool on the Hill*." - Craig Ferguson

* * * * *

"Vice President Joe Biden is on a trip to Bosnia, Serbia, and Kosovo. The White House is calling it 'Operation Keep Joe Biden Away From the Microphones.'" - Jay Leno

* * * * *

"Hey, I thought this was nice. To celebrate Earth Day, a group of schoolchildren in Washington each planted a hair plug in Joe Biden's head." - Jay Leno

* * * * *

"Today was Joe Biden's first full day as Vice President. Yeah, advisors say Biden spent most of the day watering his hair." - Conan O'Brien

* * * * *

"It's Vice President-elect Joe Biden's birthday today. And Barack Obama bought him 12 cupcakes for his birthday, which is a smart gift to give Biden because when his mouth is full of cupcakes he can't say anything stupid." - Craig Ferguson

* * * * *

"And as you know, they've already come out with a Sarah Palin action figure. And today, the Democrats released a Joe Biden action figure. It talks and talks and talks. You just can't get the thing to shut up." - Jay Leno

* * * * *

"In fact, the other day while talking to a group of supporters, Joe Biden said that Hillary Clinton might have been a better pick for vice president than him. Well, that's one thing to get the base fired up. Tell them they picked the wrong person! Yeah! That'll get them fired up!" - Jay Leno

* * * * *

"Joe Biden is Barack Obama's running mate. Yeah, nothing says 'change' like a guy who's been in the Senate for 35 years!" - David Letterman

* * * * *

Despite all the animosity in this campaign John McCain and Joe Biden are actually old friends from the Senate. They've been friends for years. In fact, they go back so far that when they first met, McCain had hair, and Biden didn't.

* * * * *

"Joe Biden, on the day of announcing his candidacy for President of the United States, called Barack Obama 'the first mainstream African-American who is articulate, bright and clean.' I think we've seen the shortest presidential campaign in history." - Jay Leno

* * * * *

"In a speech in Washington, D.C., Delaware Senator Joe Biden said although he wants to be president, he'd rather be at home making love to his wife. Which is ironic, because Bill Clinton said the same thing. He said he'd rather be home making love to Joe Biden's wife too." - Jay Leno

* * * * *

Barack Obama has chosen Delaware Senator Joseph Biden as his running mate. Well, Biden has 35 years of experience in Washington. So between the two of them, that's almost *36* years of experience.

* * * * *

"Did you hear Joe Biden is in the process of writing his autobiography? It's called *Iacocca*." - Biden lost his credibility during the 1988 presidential race when he was caught plagiarizing a speech.

SLICK WILLIE

The Clintons were driving through Arkansas, and needing gas they pulled over. Hillary excused herself to go to the ladies' room, and after filling the tank Bill went looking for Hillary and was surprised to see her talking animatedly with the gas station attendant. Stunned, he watched as she gave the attendant a big hug and a kiss on each cheek.

"What was that all about?" Bill asked huffily when she returned to the car.

"Oh," explained Hillary, "I went to high school with that guy. In fact, I think I even dated him at one time, so we were catching up on old times."

"Well," observed Bill, "I guess you're glad you married me, because otherwise you'd be with a guy who pumps gas for a living."

"Oh no, Bill," said Hillary, "if I had married him, today *he'd* be the President of the United States!"

* * * * *

Top 10 Chapter Titles in Bill Clinton's Memoirs

10. "I'm Writing This Chapter Naked."

9. "I Pray Hillary Doesn't Read Pages 6, 18, 41-49, 76 And Everything Past 200."

8. "Protecting The Constitution: How To Get Gravy Stains Out Of The Parchment."

7. "A Few Of My Favorite Subpoenas."

6. "From Gennifer to Paula to Monica: Why It Pays To Keep Lowering Your Standards."

5. "1995-1998: The Extra-Pasty Years."

4. "Kneel To The Chief."

3. "What's The Deal With That Moron You Guys Replaced Me With?"

2. "NAFTA - Bringing America Into... Ah Screw That, Who Wants to Read Some More About Bubba Gettin' Down?"

1. "The Night I Accidentally Slept With Hillary."

* * * * *

"It appears there's a HUGE typographical error on the cover of Bill Clinton's new book, *My Life*. Somebody mistakenly inserted an 'F' in the title."
- Chuck Muth

* * * * *

"President Clinton will be moving out of the White House next week, and when he does he is expected to be the first President in history not to get his security deposit back." - SNL Weekend Update anchor Jimmy Fallon

* * * * *

"John Kerry made a mistake of saying something embarrassing while a microphone was on. And now he's been backpedaling. So now he's hired a guy, and his sole job is to make sure John Kerry's microphone is off. It's the same guy that used to watch Clinton's fly." - David Letterman

* * * * *

"The Israelis know that if the Iraqi or Iranian army came across the Jordan River, I would personally grab a rifle, get in a ditch and fight and die."- Draft dodger Bill Clinton at a Jewish fundraiser in Toronto

* * * * *

"Playing saxophone at the grand opening of the Mohegan Sun Casino was Bill Clinton - or, as the Indians call him, 'Dances with Cows.'" - Craig Kilborn

* * * * *

"Talking about Bill Clinton, yesterday the Supreme Court disbarred him, but he's not worried about that, because he's just going to pardon himself."
- David Letterman

* * * * *

Q. What do you get when you cross a crooked politician with a dishonest lawyer?
A. Chelsea Clinton

* * * * *

President and Laura Bush sent out a record *two million* Christmas cards this year. By comparison, President Clinton only sent half a million Christmas cards but, to be fair, he *did* send out nearly five million Valentines.

* * * * *

On the eve of the 1996 election Liz Dole said to Hillary Clinton, "I slept with the future President of the United States last night," to which Mrs. Clinton responded, "That Bill will do *anything* for a vote."

* * * * *

"[Clinton] claims he was banished to an actual couch in a living room next to their bedroom, for two months. Is that really true? In that summer of 1998, when he was lobbing cruise missiles at abandoned Osama training camps in Afghanistan, the President was doing so on the basis of a couple of hours' tossing on the couch? If you say so. Today, of course, the Clintons are back sleeping together, even if only at the Reagan funeral." -Mark Steyn

* * * * *

"When [attention is] focused elsewhere, as when President George W. Bush was eulogizing Ronald Reagan, [Clinton] slipped into slumber. Was [he] napping, or was he privately projecting his own future state funeral and famous last words?"

Let's compare the two:

Ronald Reagan: "Mr. Gorbachev, tear down this wall."

Bill Clinton: "I did not have sex with that woman, Ms. Lewinsky."

-Kathleen Parker

* * * * *

Out of habit, Clinton vehemently denied ever writing his memoirs... It was also the first time an interview with a former President contained the phrase "booty call." - One of the top surprises in Bill Clinton's actual *60 Minutes* Interview

* * * * *

"President Bush was in Little Rock Tuesday to hail the success of his 'No Child Left Behind' policy in Arkansas. Bill Clinton would never have made a speech like that. People there are still debating how many children *he* left behind in Arkansas." –Argus Hamilton

* * * * *

A man was shopping in a supermarket in Chappaqua, New York during the final days of the Clinton administration. As he came around the corner of the dairy aisle he bumped into someone. It turned out to be none other than Bill Clinton himself, who was in town to look at houses.

The man was so shocked all he could blurt out was "Pardon me, Mr. President!"

Clinton thought about it for a moment and said, "Sure, why not. What's one more?"

* * * * *

"Clinton told Dan Rather last night that the worst day of his life was the 'day he told Hillary the truth.' So he's not going to do that again... Nope, not gonna make *that* mistake! – Jay Leno

* * * * *

Bill Clinton, George Bush, Barack Obama and Ronald Reagan were on an ocean liner when it began to sink.

Reagan said, "Quick, let's get everyone to the lifeboats."

Bush said, "Women and children first."

Obama said, "Screw the women and children."

Clinton said, "Do you think we have time?"

* * * * *

"John Kerry is recovering nicely after having prostate surgery. But the doctors did tell him it would be several months before he could be sexually active again. All the other Democratic candidates have been very supportive. Joe Lieberman called to wish him the best. The Reverend Al Sharpton called to offer prayers. Former President Bill Clinton called Mrs. Kerry and asked if she was lonely." – Jay Leno

* * * * *

"Clinton discussed his affair with Monica Lewinsky and said, 'I did something for the worst possible reason, just because I could.' What *else* was he going to say? I had no choice... she outweighed me. She pinned me down!" – Jay Leno

* * * * *

"An Internet rumor claims that John Kerry had an affair with a young woman. When asked if this was similar to the Clinton-Lewinsky scandal, a spokesman said 'Close, but no cigar.'" - Jimmy Fallon, on Saturday Night Live's "Weekend Update"

* * * * *

"President Clinton also testified before the 9/11 commission. He said he was very concerned about an attack. In fact Clinton said he couldn't remember how many times he had told women in the White House, 'Just keep your head down.'" - Jay Leno

* * * * *

"I think that Clinton was a little confused when he appeared before the 9/11 commission. He kept telling them, 'I did not have sexual relations with Osama Bin Laden.'" - Jay Leno

* * * * *

Bill and Hillary were at Yankee Stadium for a World Series Game, and were sitting in the first row with the Secret Service detail directly behind them. Just before the start of the game one of the Secret Service guys leaned forward and said something to the President. Clinton stared at the guy, looked at Hillary, looked back at the agent, and shook his head violently.

The agent then said, "Mr. President, it was a unanimous request, from the owner of the team down to the bat boy. And the fans would love it!"

So Bill shrugged his shoulders and said, "Okay then, if that's what the people want."

He got up, grabbed Hillary by her collar and the seat of her pants, and dropped her right over the wall onto the field. She got up kicking, swearing, and screaming, and the crowd went wild! For several minutes they continued cheering, applauding, and high-fiving.

Bill was bowing and smiling, and leaned over to the agent and said, "You were right, I would have never believed that!"

Then he noticed the agent has gone totally pale, and asked what was wrong.

The agent replied, "Sir, I said they wanted you to throw out the first *PITCH!*"

* * * * *

"Former President Bill Clinton says he lost so much weight on his new diet he has to get all new clothes. At least that's what he told Hillary when she caught him with his pants down... again." - Jay Leno

* * * * *

"Former President Clinton went to London to see Chelsea and meet her new boyfriend. I guess the boyfriend told Clinton he thought of him as a role model. Clinton said, "That's it - you are *not* dating my daughter!'" - Jay Leno

* * * * *

When asked what he thought about foreign affairs, Clinton replied, "I don't know, I never had one."

* * * * *

"Congressman Anthony Weiner called former President Bill Clinton to apologize about his sex scandal. WHAT? Apologize for what... copyright infringement?" – Jon Stewart on the *Daily Show*

* * * * *

The Clinton revised judicial oath: "I solemnly swear to tell the truth as I know it, the whole truth as I believe it to be, and nothing but what I think you need to know."

* * * * *

"Producers of the game show *Hollywood Squares* said that they have asked former President Bill Clinton to be the center square on the show, and Clinton is considering it. How humbling is that? The same week that Jimmy Carter gets the Nobel Peace Prize, you are asked to be the center square!" - Jay Leno

* * * * *

Chrysler Corporation is adding a new car to its line to honor Bill Clinton. The *Dodge Drafter* will be in production in Canada this year!

* * * * *

According to a number of leading Presidential historians, Bill Clinton lacked only three things to become one of America's finest leaders: integrity, vision, and wisdom!

* * * * *

Clinton will be recorded in history as the only President to do Hanky Panky between the Bushes.

* * * * *

"Can you believe there's only two days left in the Clinton administration? Boy, time flies when you're having sex." - Jay Leno

* * * * *

"Hell, if you work for Bill Clinton, you go up and down more times than a whore's nightgown." - James Carville

* * * * *

"I certainly wouldn't want any unneutered Clintons in my house." - Former Labor Secretary nominee Linda Chavez, wondering about the reproductive status of Socks the cat, whom she has offered to adopt

* * * * *

"He (Bill Clinton) has got a scandalous past and he's talking about how much he's going to love being the (Senate) spouse's club. Do you think that makes the male senators feel good? Do you think Senator Orrin Hatch right now is sleeping easy? Do you think Lieberman doesn't think Clinton is going to be sidling on up to Hadassah in the Senate club: 'Can I buy you a Manischevitz?' Believe me, they're nervous." - Jon Stewart

* * * * *

"It's the first time Clinton has ever rejected p---y in his life." - G. Gordon Liddy, on reports that the Clintons were giving away First Cat Socks to Betty Currie

* * * * *

"President Clinton made a deal so he wouldn't be prosecuted... not only that, all the sex charges against him have been plea-bargained down to practicing gynecology without a license." - Jay Leno

* * * * *

"Here's a great rumor. According to the *Drudge Report*, NBC is in discussions with President Clinton about developing a talk show for him on their network. It will be like *Meet the Press*, except with Clinton it will be called *Press the Meat*." - Jay Leno

* * * * *

"We make a lot of fun at President Clinton's expense, but this transition is going to be tough for him because it's been 25 years since this guy has gotten laid in the private sector." - David Letterman

* * * * *

"In just two weeks, Bill Clinton will no longer be President of the United States. He'll just be another chubby, middle-aged guy annoying the waitresses at Hooters." - Jay Leno

* * * * *

"I may not have been the greatest president, but I've had the most fun eight years!" - Bill Clinton

* * * * *

"Clinton is saying he's going to model his after-presidential life after Jimmy Carter. He'll be doing a lot of hammering and a lot of nailing, but he ain't building houses." - David Letterman

* * * * *

"If the dress doesn't fit, we must acquit. If it's on the dress, he must confess." - Congressman James Traficant

* * * * *

"The president looked me in the eye and told me the same thing on several occasions. And I'm not upset. You want to know why? Because I never believed him in the first place." – Democratic Senator Robert Torricelli, on Bill Clinton's denials of an affair with Monica Lewinsky

* * * * *

"I've learned not to put things in my mouth that are bad for me." - Monica Lewinsky, on CNN's Larry King Live discussing her miraculous Jenny Craig weight-loss.

* * * * *

"You know, if I were a single man, I might ask that mummy out. That's a good-looking mummy." - Bill Clinton, looking at "Juanita," a newly discovered Incan mummy on display at the National Geographic museum

* * * * *

"Probably she does look good compared to the mummy he's been f%&king." - Press Secretary Mike McCurry, making an off-the-cuff joke to reporters

* * * * *

"Bill Clinton is everywhere now promoting his new book. I believe the last time Clinton did a media blitz like this it was to *deny* everything that's *in* this book." - David Letterman

* * * * *

"Bill Clinton's book went on sale today at long last. Earlier today hundreds of people waited outside of Barnes and Noble in the pouring rain for a chance to meet him. When asked if she minded the rain, one woman said, 'I'm meeting Bill Clinton. I just *assumed* my dress would get ruined.'" - Conan O'Brien

* * * * *

"How many of you folks purchased a copy of *My Life* by Bill Clinton? It was in the book stores yesterday, and it was a great day for Bill. The first day out he sold 1,500 books and he got six phone numbers." - David Letterman

* * * * *

"I just read Bill Clinton's book. Hundreds of affairs, thousands of lies, lawsuits, subpoenas… and then I got to page two." - Craig Kilborn

* * * * *

"I loved it when Bill Clinton told Dan Rather the worst day of his life was the day he told Hillary the truth. Well, of course, it was. The first time you try *anything* it's always going to be difficult." - Jay Leno

* * * * *

"Bill Clinton, they now are saying has got nothing to do. So every night he goes to a bar there in Chappaqua and Clinton says that he really enjoys spending time in the bar because the more he drinks, every woman starts to look like Paula Jones." - David Letterman

* * * * *

"President Bush welcomed Bill and Hillary Clinton back to the White House for the unveiling of Bill's official portrait. There are two firsts involved. It's the first presidential portrait ever painted by an African-American artist, and it's the very first presidential portrait to feature full-frontal nudity."
- Jay Leno

* * * * *

"This weekend 1,000 people lined up at Barnes and Noble to see Bill Clinton. Not to buy his book, but to give him a Father's Day card." - Craig Kilborn

* * * * *

"It's (Bill Clinton's book) actually longer than the new Harry Potter book. And both of them, I believe, are about a boy and his wand." - David Letterman

* * * * *

Bill Clinton steps out onto the White House lawn in the dead of winter.

Right in front of him, on the White House lawn, he sees "The President Must Go" written in urine across the snow.

Well, old Bill is pretty ticked off. He storms into his security staff's HQ and yells, "Somebody wrote a threat in the snow on the front damn lawn! And they wrote it in urine! The son-of-a-bitch had to be standing right on the porch when he did it! Where were you guys?!"

The security guys stay silent and stare ashamedly at the floor.

Bill hollers, "Well dammit, don't just sit there! Get out and FIND OUT WHO DID IT! I want an answer, and I want it TONIGHT!"

The entire staff immediately jumps up and races for the exits. Later that evening, his chief security officer approaches him and says, "Well Mr. President, we have some bad news and we have some really bad news. Which do you want first?"

Clinton says, "Oh hell, give me the bad news first."

The officer says, "Well, we took a sample of the urine and tested it. The results just came back, and it was Al Gore`s urine."

Clinton says, "Oh my god, I feel so... so... betrayed! My own Vice President! Damn...well, what`s the *really* bad news?"

The officer replies, "Well sir, it was Hillary's handwriting!"

* * * * *

Q. What does Bill say to Hillary after a romantic interlude?
A. "I'll be home in 20 minutes!"

* * * * *

Q. Why is Clinton so interested in events in the Middle East?
A. He thinks the Gaza Strip is a topless bar.

UNCLE TEDDY

You will only understand the symbolism of the following if you know that Ted Kennedy drove off of a bridge in Chappaquiddick, Massachusetts on his way to an island with Mary Joe Kopechne in the late 60s. He did NOT seek help to rescue her when he surfaced, but instead made his way to a hotel, called friends and the next morning reported the accident. She was, needless to say, both dead and wet. Kennedy received no censure or reprimand, much less any legal punishment for this negligent act of manslaughter. Kennedy power extends wide in that part of America... so you have got to love the chutzpah of Rumsfeld!

Defense Secretary Donald Rumsfeld told Senator Edward M. Kennedy that he was "all wet" at a Senate Armed Services Committee hearing when the Senator alleged that the Bush administration had lied about Iraq's weapons of mass destruction to justify going to war.

Kennedy began his questioning of Rumsfeld by saying, "Don't you think the Bush administration should be held legally accountable for the lies it told about Iraqi weapons, and the subsequent cover-up?"

"First, with all due respect Senator Kennedy, you're all wet," said Rumsfeld. "The administration has not lied or covered up. However, in general, I do believe that when a man commits a crime he should face the bar of justice. He should not be allowed to serve in positions of power in our government, and be hailed as a leader, when the question of his guilt remains unresolved, if you know what I mean."

"I'm sure I do not know what you mean," Kennedy said, "but the American people deserve to know why you can't find Saddam's weapons of mass destruction."

"Sometimes things are hard to find, even when you know where they are," said Rumsfeld. "For example, I've heard of a man who missed a bridge and drove his car into the water, even though he knew where the bridge was. And then sometimes you just keep diving into a problem and despite repeated efforts, you come up empty handed. That doesn't mean that nothing's there. As you know, eventually, the truth comes to light."

Having no further questions, Senator Kennedy yielded the remainder of his time.

* * * * *

"The opening night of next month's Democratic convention in Boston is set to feature an emotional party tribute to hometown hero Ted Kennedy, who has served in office longer than every other senator but one. Guess no one at the Democratic National Committee took a close look at the calendar: That July 26 salute to Teddy just happens to coincide with the 35th anniversary of Chappaquiddick."
- *New York Post* columnist Eric Fettmann

* * * * *

The Kerry folks asked the local priest last Sunday to mention in his homily that Kerry is a saint. The priest, a devout Catholic, agreed and began his homily by saying, "John Kerry is a crook. John Kerry is a liar. John Kerry is a fraud. John Kerry is an adulterer. John Kerry is one of the worst Catholics I have ever met... *but* compared to Ted Kennedy - he's a saint!"

* * * * *

Q: What was Gary Hart's biggest mistake?
A: Not letting Teddy Kennedy drive Donna Rice home!

* * * * *

"Ted Kennedy is endorsing John Kerry and I'm wondering, do you really want the endorsement of a guy with a permanent Bloody Mary mustache?"
- David Letterman

* * * * *

"It's 'Bring Your Daughter to Work Day.' This tradition was begun about 25 years ago down in Washington, D.C. by a quick-thinking Ted Kennedy, who was spotted leaving his office with an 18-year-old." - David Letterman

* * * * *

"On Wednesday, President Bush named the Justice Department headquarters after Robert F. Kennedy. Then he went around the corner and named a strip club after Ted." - Jay Leno

* * * * *

Q: What did Ted Kennedy have that Bill Clinton *wishes* he had??
A: An ex-wife, and a dead girlfriend!

* * * * *

Q: What made Ted Kennedy cry during sex?
A: Mace

* * * * *

"After the Jeffords switch, the Democrats would have 51 seats, the Republicans would have 49 seats, and Senator Ted Kennedy would still need *four* seats." - Craig Kilborn

* * * * *

In the early 70's, when Volkswagen still sold their beetle in the USA, they were fond of bragging about how airtight they were. One of their ads even showed a beetle floating in the middle of a pond. *National Lampoon* ran the same picture with the caption: "If Ted Kennedy had driven a Volkswagen, he'd be president today!" When a lawsuit was threatened by VW, *National Lampoon* ran the following retraction: "Even if Ted Kennedy *had* driven a Volkswagen, he wouldn't be president today!"

* * * * *

"Politically, the big news is now this guy Senator Jim Jeffords from Vermont announced late yesterday he's changing parties and no longer going to be a Republican, thinking maybe an independent, so he's changing parties. But you know, it's not unusual for senators to change party. For example, last night Ted Kennedy went from a party at Bennigan's to a party at Houlihan's." - David Letterman

* * * * *

"Senator Jeffords says the reason he's leaving the Republican party is he's just fed up with George Bush and the tax cuts and he's also fed up with his environmental policy. But the big reason, he says, is Ted Kennedy and the Democrats offered to let him get in on some of that hot intern action." - David Letterman

FLIPPER

"Everyone is waiting to see if this left-wing radio thing will be successful. See, I think it's a good idea. I think we should consider different points of view. Like me, I like to hear both sides of an issue. That's why I listen to John Kerry. I know sooner or later, I'll get both sides of an issue. In fact, today John Kerry finally cleared up his position on military action in Iraq. He said he voted yes on shock, no on awe." - Jay Leno

* * * * *

TOP TEN REASONS KERRY RAN FOR PRESIDENT

10. To bring renewed tedium and uncertainty to the Democratic party.

9. To be the greatest horse-faced President since Polk.

8. Couldn't live with himself if he didn't hold a higher office than Schwarzenegger.

7. Needed an excuse to get out of a wedding in February.

6. Get elected, eat a ton of waffles, become the fattest President.

5. Long days on the campaign trail beat sitting around being nagged by the wife to put away the socks.

4. An unusually persuasive horoscope told him he should.

3. Did you know if the President kills some guy in a bar fight, the FBI will make it cool?

2. A leader who supports both sides of every issue is a friend to all Americans.

1. To show the world not all Democrats are ass-grabbing womanizers.

* * * * *

"Yesterday Senator John Kerry changed his mind and now supports the ban on gay marriages. I'm telling you, this guy has more positions than Paris Hilton." - David Letterman

* * * * *

"We make jokes about it, but the truth is this presidential election really offers us a choice of two well-informed opposing positions on every issue. Okay, they both belong to John Kerry, but they're still there." - Jay Leno

* * * * *

"The Secret Service has announced it is doubling its protection for John Kerry. You can understand why - with two positions on every issue, he has twice as many people mad at him." - Jay Leno

* * * * *

"John Kerry has a new campaign slogan, 'A mind is a terrible thing to change all the time.'" - Jay Leno

* * * * *

"John Kerry met with Ralph Nader last week. Both sides of every issue were discussed. And then, Nader spoke." - Jay Leno

* * * * *

"John Kerry fell off of his bicycle over the weekend. He went for a Sunday afternoon ride, and fell off in front of the news media. Luckily, his hair broke the fall so it's not as serious. Thankfully, Senator Kerry was not seriously injured. In fact when the police arrived, Kerry was well enough to give conflicting reports to the officers about what happened." - Jay Leno

* * * * *

"Kerry has already begun his search for a running mate. They say that because John Edwards still has $50 million in campaign money, Kerry might pick him. Pick him? Hey, for $50 million, Kerry will *marry* him." - Jay Leno

* * * * *

"They had a profile of John Kerry on the news and they said his first wife was worth around $300 million and his second wife, his current wife, is worth around $700 million. So when John Kerry says he's going after the wealthy in this country, he's not just talking. He's *doing* it!" - Jay Leno

* * * * *

"John Kerry accused President Bush of catering to the rich. You know, as opposed to John Kerry, who just *marries* them." - Jay Leno

* * * * *

John Kerry has called for an increase in the minimum wage. He said people out there are struggling, and you can't *always* fix the problem by marrying a rich woman!

* * * * *

"There was an embarrassing moment at a recent Democratic fundraiser. When John Kerry was handed a $10 million dollar check, he said, 'I do.'"
- Craig Kilborn

* * * * *

"Teresa Heinz is on the cover of *Newsweek* magazine. John Kerry said he first noticed her when she was on the cover of another magazine - *Fortune*." - Jay Leno

* * * * *

"They say John Kerry is the first Democratic presidential candidate in history to raise $50 million in a three-month period. Actually, that's nothing. He once raised $500 million with two words: 'I do.'"
-Jay Leno

* * * * *

"John Kerry has promised to take this country back from the wealthy. Who better than the guy worth $700 million to take the country back? See, he knows how the wealthy think. He can spy on them at his country club, at his place in Palm Beach, at his house in the Hamptons. He's like a mole for the working man." - Jay Leno

* * * * *

"John Kerry will be the Democratic nominee for president. Democrats finally found someone who is Al Gore, without the flash and the sizzle." - Craig Kilborn

* * * * *

"Bill Clinton has a brand new book coming out in a few months, and the Democrats are worried that the Clinton book might upstage the Kerry campaign. I'm thinking, *day-old meat loaf* could upstage that campaign!" - David Letterman

* * * * *

"John Kerry had shoulder surgery this week, and he needed no anesthesia. He just listened to one of his speeches." - David Letterman

* * * * *

"John Kerry and Ralph Nader met face-to-face. It was a historic meeting. Astronomers said today their meeting actually created what is called a 'charisma black hole.'" - Jay Leno

* * * * *

During a campaign tour of the Apache Nation Wednesday, Democratic presidential candidate John Kerry said he had a plan to increase every Native American's income by $40,000 a year. Senator Kerry refused repeated requests for details of his plan, however. He also told the Apaches that during his Senate career, he has voted YES 9,637 times for every Indian issue ever introduced.

Before his departure, the Apache Tribe presented the Presidential candidate a plaque inscribed with his new Indian name, Running Eagle.

After Kerry left, tribal officials explained that Running Eagle is a bird so full of sh#t it can't fly.

* * * * *

"During the first Democratic presidential debate Howard Dean started off by apologizing to the crowd for having a cold. Then John Kerry apologized for once having a cold while serving his country in Vietnam." - Conan O'Brien

* * * * *

The most grating thing about Kerry is the way he works the fact that he went to Vietnam into every conversation. You could be talking to him about snow cones and he'd say, "They didn't have any snow cones in Vietnam." If you brought up the Redskins, he'd tell you, "I had a friend back in Nam who was a big Redskins fan." Even if you told him to talk about anything except Vietnam he'd say, "So I can't talk about Vietnam huh? No Vietnam at all... hmmm. Wow, without talking about my service in Vietnam, I have nothing to talk about."

* * * * *

When Kerry got back from Vietnam he PROTESTED against the war and claimed to have thrown his medals over the White House fence (yes, he lied). Then later on in 1992, Kerry defended Bill Clinton from Vietnam vet Bob Kerrey by saying, "I am saddened by the fact that Vietnam has yet again been inserted into the campaign, and that it has been inserted in what I feel to be the worst possible way... What saddens me most is that Democrats, above all those who shared the agonies of that generation, should now be re-fighting the many conflicts of Vietnam in order to win the current political conflict of a presidential primary."

* * * * *

"The White House began airing their TV commercials to re-elect the president, and the John Kerry campaign is condemning his use of 9/11 in the ads. He said it is unconscionable to use the tragic memory of a war in order to get elected unless, of course, it's the *Vietnam* War." - Jay Leno

* * * * *

"The Democrats are all over this. Democratic strategists feel John Kerry's war record means he can beat Bush. They say when it comes down to it, voters will *always* vote for a war hero over someone who tried to get out of the war. I'll be sure to mention that to Bob Dole (who lost to draft dodger Bill Clinton) when I see him." - Jay Leno

* * * * *

"According to a new study, Botox injections can help back pain. So you see, that's why John Kerry had all that Botox - his back was killing him from all that flip-flopping on issues." - Jay Leno

* * * * *

"I'm worried about John Kerry. He's so confident now that he's already planning his White House sex scandal." - David Letterman

* * * * *

"In a new issue of *Esquire* magazine, they revealed that before he was married to Teresa Heinz, Senator John Kerry dated Morgan Fairchild, Michelle Phillips, Catherine Oxenberg and Dana Delany. Finally, a Democratic presidential candidate with *good* taste in women." - Jay Leno

* * * * *

"The Presidential campaign is getting kind of ugly. Did you hear about this? Yesterday, a 27-year-old woman came forth to deny rumors that she had an affair with Democratic front-runner John Kerry. The woman added, 'I would *never* cheat on Bill Clinton!'" - Conan O'Brien

* * * * *

"In his big victory speech last night, Senator Kerry said that he wanted to defeat George Bush and the 'economy of privilege.' Then he hugged his wife, Teresa, heir to the multi-million dollar Heinz food fortune." - Jay Leno

* * * * *

"Kerry said today that he wants to get rid of tax cuts for the rich and his wife said, 'Hey, shut up! What's the matter with you?! Are you nuts?!'" - Jay Leno

* * * * *

"It really kind of looks like now that John Kerry is on his way to the presidential nomination. The only thing that can sink Kerry now is an Al Gore endorsement." - Jay Leno

* * * * *

"A new poll shows that Senator Kerry's support in the South is strongest amongst blacks. Kerry's appeal to Southern blacks is obvious. He is an ultra-liberal, ultra-wealthy white man who lives far, far away." - Dennis Miller

* * * * *

"The big winner on Super Tuesday was Senator John Kerry. He won 39 percent of the vote, which is pretty good, and begs the question... why the long face?" - Jay Leno

* * * * *

"John Kerry said that a lot of world leaders want him to be the president, and the Bush administration said, 'Yeah, well, like who?' and John Kerry said, 'Well, I can't say really.' So now they're really hammering John Kerry, and listen to this - the only name he could come up with was Queen Latifah."
- David Letterman

* * * * *

"Please, John Kerry, stop rolling up your sleeves like you're about to man a register at Costco. You're a Boston Brahmin who married not one, but two eccentric heiresses. You're not Joe Sixpack. You're Claus Von Bulow." - Bill Maher

* * * * *

"In his speech last night, John Kerry said this was the beginning of the end of the Bush administration. I agree. Sure, it may take another five years, but this is it." - Jay Leno

* * * * *

"Well, the good news for Democrats is now over half the country can identify a picture of John Kerry. The bad news, the majority still thinks he's the dad from *The Munsters*." - Jay Leno

* * * * *

"John Kerry was in Florida this week, reaching out and talking with elderly voters. You know, I think it made Kerry a little uncomfortable to be with these elderly people. He finally got a chance to see what he'd look like without Botox." - Jay Leno

* * * * *

"The head of the AFL-CIO endorsed John Kerry, saying, 'The time has come to get behind one man, one leader, one candidate.' Then he said, 'And until we *find* that man, we will endorse John Kerry.'"
- Conan O'Brien

* * * * *

"John Kerry has apologized for saying those who do not study hard and do their homework will get stuck in Iraq, because he now realizes those that do not campaign well and are boring will end up stuck in the Senate." - Jay Leno

* * * * *

"Big story, of course, is John Kerry finally apologized. Some political analysts are now saying that Senator John Kerry's botched joke about the troops hurt his chances of becoming president in 2008. Apparently, Kerry's chances of becoming president went from zero, to less than zero." - Conan O'Brien

* * * * *

"John Kerry went hunting today. He said he killed a goose. He didn't bring Teresa along because he was a little rusty and he was afraid he might kill the goose that laid the golden egg." - Jay Leno

* * * * *

"On Wednesday, he said he wouldn't apologize. On Thursday, he apologized. Today, he said, 'It doesn't matter. It just feels great to be flip-flopping again.'"
- Bill Maher

* * * * *

"John Kerry went duck hunting and he's doing that to fulfill his campaign pledge to hunt down the ducks and kill them wherever they are! Kerry did pretty well. He came back with four ducks, and three Purple Hearts." - David Letterman

* * * * *

"Kerry scored many points with voters and pundits by finally putting to rest criticism that he's a flip-flopper. Kerry said, 'I have one position on Iraq: I'm forgainst it." - Amy Pohler, *Saturday Night Live's* "Weekend Update"

* * * * *

"Of course, I would support Bush over Kerry even if we weren't at war, because Bush is the more conservative candidate... plus, I'm not on crack!"
- Jonah Goldberg

BILLARY

The United States Postal Service created a stamp with a picture of Hillary Clinton to honor her achievements as First Lady of our nation, but in daily use it was shown that the stamp was not sticking to envelopes. This enraged Hillary, who demanded a full investigation, and after months of testing a special presidential commission made the following findings: The stamp was in perfect order, and there was nothing wrong with the applied adhesive. People were just spitting on the wrong side.

* * * * *

Top Ten Signs Hillary Wants To Be President

10. The Washington, D.C. TJ Maxx has sold out of pantsuits.

9. She's practicing sitting around doing nothing.

8. Instead of pretending to be from New York, she's pretending to be from key battleground states Ohio, Florida and Michigan.

7. She bragged to reporters the next "Hillary-Gate" is going to be off the hizzook.

6. She says she wants to be the first female President since Jimmy Carter.

5. She just purchased a very large amount of Halliburton stock.

4. She called Century 21 to ask about listings for undisclosed locations.

3. Well, there's the "Obama/Clinton" tattoo.

2. She firing up the ol' paper shredder.

1. If it would help, she'd have sex with Bill.

* * * * *

DEAR ABBY

Dear Abby:

My husband is a liar and a cheat. He has cheated on me from the beginning, and when I confront him, he denies everything. What's worse, everyone *knows* he cheats on me. It is so humiliating.

Also, since he lost his job four years ago he hasn't even looked for a new one. All he does is buy cigars and cruise around chitchatting with his pals, while I have to work to pay the bills. Since our daughter went away to college he doesn't even pretend to like me, and hints that I am a lesbian. What should I do?

Signed,

Clueless

Dear Clueless:

Grow up and dump him. For Pete's sake, you don't need him anymore – after all, you're Secretary of State, and a former United States Senator from New York. Act like it!

* * * * *

George and Laura Bush and Bill and Hillary Clinton were traveling by train to the Super Bowl. At the station George and Laura each bought a ticket and watched as Bill and Hillary purchased just one.

"How are the two of you going to travel on only one ticket?" asked George, astonished at what he was seeing.

"Watch and learn," answered Hillary.

They all board the train. George and Laura took their respective seats, but Bill and Hillary crammed into a toilet together and closed the door.

Shortly after the train has departed, the conductor comes around collecting tickets.

He knocked on the toilet door and said, "Ticket, please." The door opened just a crack and a single arm emerged with a ticket in hand. The conductor took it, and moved on.

The Bushes saw this happen and agreed it was quite a clever idea, so after the game they decide to try a similar plan on the return trip.

When they got to the station they saw the Clintons at the window buying a single ticket for the return trip, and to their astonishment the Clintons noticed that the Bushes didn't buy any ticket at all.

"Aren't you taking a terrible chance by traveling without a ticket?" said Hillary.

"Live and learn," answered Laura.

When they boarded the train the Bushes crammed themselves into a toilet, and the Clintons crammed into another toilet just down the way. Shortly after the train lefts the station George left their toilet, walked over to the Clinton's toilet, knocked on their door and said, "Ticket, please."

* * * * *

Hillary Clinton went to a primary school in New York to talk about the world. After her talk, she offered question time.

One little boy put up his hand, and the Senator asked him what his name was.

"Kenny."

"And what is your question, Kenny?"

"I have three questions:

First - whatever happened to your medical health care plan?

Second - why would you run for President after your husband shamed the office?

And third - whatever happened to all those things you took when you left the White House?"

Just then the bell rang for recess, and Hillary informed the kiddies that they would continue after recess.

When they resumed Hillary said, "Okay where were we? Oh, that's right, question time. Who has a question?"

A different little boy put his hand up, and Hillary pointed him out and asked what his name was.

"Larry."

"And what is your question, Larry?"

"Actually, I have five questions:

First - whatever happened to your medical health care plan?

Second - why would you run for President after your husband shamed the office?

Third - whatever happened to all those things you took when you left the White House?

Fourth - why did the recess bell go off twenty minutes early?

And fifth - what happened to Kenny?"

* * * * *

In 2008 someone finally came out with a 100% bipartisan political bumper sticker. It said "RUN HILLARY RUN." Democrats put it on the rear bumper, and Republicans put it on the front!

* * * * *

"A student from the University of Washington has sold his soul on eBay for $400. He's a law student, so he probably doesn't need it, but still, that's not very much. Today Hillary Clinton said, 'Hey, at least I got some furniture and a Senate seat for mine." - Jay Leno

* * * * *

One day Bill Clinton was walking along a street in Washington D.C. when a hooker waved and said "Fifty dollars!"

Clinton yelled back, "Five dollars," and the prostitute immediately rolled her eyes in disgust and walked away.

A few days later Clinton was out walking again when he spotted the same hooker on a street corner. He waved at her and once again yelled, "Five dollars!"

She flipped him the bird, yelled "Cheapskate!" and walked off.

About a week later Clinton was walking along the same street, but this time Hillary was with him. He glanced around nervously, hoping not to run into the hooker, but sure enough when they turned the corner she was standing right in front of him.

Before Clinton could say a word the hooker laughed, pointed at Hillary and said, "See what you *get* for five dollars!"

* * * * *

"Hillary Clinton is the junior senator from the great state of New York. When they swore her in, she used the Clinton family Bible. You know, the one with only *seven* commandments." - David Letterman

* * * * *

"Hillary's got this huge book, it's a memoir of her life and times at the White House. In the book she wrote that when Bill told her he was having an affair, she said 'I could hardly breathe, I was gulping for air.' No, I'm sorry... that's what *Monica* said." - David Letterman

* * * * *

"In her book Hillary Clinton said she could have divorced her husband for all of his infidelities, but decided to get counseling instead. In a related story Bill Clinton announced the name of his new book is *What in the Hell Does It Take To Get This Woman To Leave Me?*" - Craig Kilborn

* * * * *

"The A&E Network has announced they are making a two hour movie about Hillary Clinton's days in the White House. Of course they haven't come up with a title yet, but these are some of the ones they are considering: *She's Too Fat, I'm Too Furious, Dude Where's My Husband?, Ken Starr Wars, Bend It Like Monica, Crouching Monica Hidden Cigar,* and *My Husband Spent Hanukkah in Monica.*" - Jay Leno

* * * * *

"Hillary Clinton has written a book - it's a 600-page memoir - of her eight years in the White House. Six hundred pages, that's amazing. Not bad for a woman who, when she was there, had no idea what was going on." - David Letterman

* * * * *

"The publisher of Hillary Clinton's memoirs, for which she received the largest book advance in history, are worried she is way behind. It's supposed to go to printers next month, but she hasn't sent them a manuscript or even given them the title yet. But in her defense, fiction is a lot harder to write. To give you an idea of how far behind she is, she's only up to Bill's 25th affair." - Jay Leno

* * * * *

"Hillary Clinton's 506-page memoir comes out next week. So much of her personality shines through that in the end, *you'll* want to sleep with an intern too!" - Craig Kilborn

* * * * *

"Did you know Bill and Hillary Clinton were born under the same sign? Know what sign? 'FOR SALE.'" - Jay Leno

* * * * *

"Last night, Senator Hillary Clinton hosted her first party in her new home in Washington. People said it was a lot like the parties she used to host at the White House. In fact, even the furniture was the same." - Jay Leno

* * * * *

"In today's *New York Post* a man who went to Oxford with former President Clinton claims that at the time both he and Clinton dated a woman who turned out to be a radical lesbian. After hearing this, President Clinton said, 'Yeah, but only one of us *married* her.'" - Conan O'Brien

* * * * *

"I will give you an idea of how hot it was the other day. It was so hot, to cool off President Clinton actually got in bed with Hillary." - David Letterman

* * * * *

"CNN found that Hillary Clinton is the most admired woman in America. Women admire her because she's strong and successful, and men admire her because she allows her husband to cheat and get away with it." - Jay Leno

* * * * *

"Did you hear about Hillary Clinton's brother? It's not Hugh, it's Tony. Apparently he's got a vacation house somewhere in Pennsylvania and he gets beat up because he is having sex with somebody's fiancé. I keep thinking, Clinton is a lucky guy. It's hard to find a brother in law who has the same interests you do." - David Letterman

* * * * *

"Senator Hillary Clinton's brother Tony Rodham was beaten up by a guy who caught him having sex with his girlfriend. Where does that happen? Does that happen anywhere you don't have wheels on your house? Today Bill Clinton said he was shocked. He said he didn't know anybody on Hillary's side of the family even *had* sex." - Jay Leno

* * * * *

"In Hillary Clinton's new book Living History, Hillary details what it was like meeting Bill Clinton, falling in love with him, getting married, and living a passionate, wonderful life as husband and wife. Then on page two, the trouble starts." - Jay Leno

* * * * *

"There is a cold front moving across the country. Yeah, it's Hillary starting her book tour!" - Craig Kilborn

* * * * *

Bill Clinton got $12 Million for his memoirs. His wife Hillary got $8 million for hers. That's $20 million for memories from two people who for eight years repeatedly testified, under oath, that they couldn't remember anything.

* * * * *

Q. How does Bill Clinton keeps his beer cold when he is at a ball game?
A. He has Hillary hold it between her legs.

* * * * *

Q. How can you tell when Hillary Clinton is lying?
A. Her lips are moving.

THE RIGHT REV JESSE

One day in the future, Jesse Jackson has a heart attack and dies. He immediately goes to hell, where the devil is waiting for him.

"I don't know what to do," says the devil. "You are on my list, but I have no room for you. You definitely have to stay here, so I'll tell you what I'm going to do. I've got a couple of folks here who weren't quite as bad as you. I'll let one of them go, but you have to take their place. I'll even let YOU decide who leaves. But remember, you'll be taking their place."

Jesse thought that sounded pretty good, so the devil opened the door to the first room. In it was

Ted Kennedy along with a large pool of water. He kept diving in and surfacing, empty handed. Over, and over, and over, he dove in and surfaced with nothing. Such was his fate in hell.

"No," Jesse said. "I don't think so. I'm not a good swimmer, and I don't think I could do that all day long."

The devil led him to the door of the next room. In it was Mike Dukakis with a sledgehammer and a room full of rocks. All he did was swing that hammer, time after time after time.

"No, I've got this problem with my shoulder. I would be in constant agony if all I could do was break rocks all day," commented Jesse.

The devil opened a third door. Through it, Jesse saw Bill Clinton, lying on the floor with his arms tied over his head, and his legs restrained in a spread-eagle pose. Bent over him was Monica Lewinsky, doing what she does best.

Jesse looked at this in shocked disbelief, and finally said, "Yeah, I can handle *this*."

The devil smiled and said, "Okay Monica, you're free to go!"

* * * * *

"Jesse Jackson needs to recount his *children.*"
- a sign seen at President Bush's inauguration

* * * * *

"Jackson was carrying on his affair with Sanford while he was counseling President Clinton during the Monica Lewinsky scandal. In fact, he even brought his pregnant mistress to the White House. One can only assume it was to show off to Clinton how to *properly* destroy one's career and reputation." - Jon Stewart

* * * * *

"There was a rumor that Jesse Jackson was going to go over there (to Afghanistan) to talk with the Taliban, because apparently they were having trouble rhyming the word 'Jihad.'" - Jay Leno

* * * * *

"Jesse Jackson is on a 70-day tour in five cities. One of the problems in this country, he says, is poor people that can't make a living wage. So starting today, he's bumping up the payments he's making to his mistresses by $10,000." - Jay Leno

* * * * *

"Jesse had unselfishly volunteered to go to China to help gain the release of the U.S. soldiers. He was going to go by himself, with no security. He was going to go alone. Yes, once again, Jesse is going in without protection." - Jay Leno

109

* * * * *

"I guess we didn't even officially apologize. Jesse Jackson called on the United States to officially apologize to the Chinese. Jesse said, 'An apology is not a sign of weakness.' And as President Clinton has taught us, an apology isn't even a sign you're *sorry*." - Jay Leno

* * * * *

"Jesse Jackson's in trouble. They're going after this tax thing. Jesse said he will amend his taxes to show the money that he paid to his mistress. See, he has just one mistress, and uses the standard mistress deduction, as opposed to Clinton, who had to itemize." - Jay Leno

* * * * *

"As part of his ongoing financial disclosures, Jesse Jackson told the *Chicago Sun Times* this week that he doesn't have a checking account or a credit card. Probably because to get those, you need a job."
- Tina Fey, on *Saturday Night Live's* "Weekend Update"

* * * * *

"It gives new meaning to affirmative action. She said, 'Do you want some action?' and Jesse said, '*affirmative*.'" - Jay Leno, on Jesse Jackson's extramarital affair

* * * * *

"Reportedly Jackson paid the woman $40,000 cash to move to L.A. where she is living in a $365,000 home, and he is also paying her $10,000 a month. Apparently, this woman has found the pot of gold at the end of the Rainbow Coalition." - Jay Leno

* * * * *

"As I'm sure you know, Jesse Jackson was overheard saying, and I'll put this delicately, that he wanted to cut Barack Obama's testicles off. And Jesse has been on several news programs the last couple of days, explaining what he meant by those comments. Do you really need to explain that?" - Jay Leno

* * * * *

"Jesse Jackson also said he thought Barack Obama was talking down to black people by lecturing them on things like fatherhood and being a responsible husband. Jesse thought it was insulting, not only to him, but to his mistress and their love child." - Jay Leno

* * * * *

Jesse Jackson and Al Sharpton were visiting a primary school class and found themselves in a discussion about words and their meanings. The teacher asked them if they would like to lead a discussion of the word "tragedy," so Jesse asked the class for an example of the word.

One boy stood up and offered, "If my friend, who lives on a farm, is playing in the field and a runaway tractor knocked him dead, that would be a tragedy."

No," said Jesse, "that would be an accident."

A little girl raised her hand. "If a school bus carrying 50 children drove over a cliff, killing everyone inside, that would be a tragedy."

I'm afraid not," explained Reverend Al. "That's what we would call a great loss."

The room went silent, and no other children volunteered. Sharpton searched the room. "Isn't there someone here who can give me an example of a tragedy?"

Finally at the back of the room little Johnny raised his hand. In a stern voice he said, "If a plane carrying the Reverends Jackson and Sharpton were struck by a missile and blown to smithereens that would be a tragedy."

Fantastic!" exclaimed the Reverends. "That's right. And can you tell me why that would be a tragedy?"

"Well," says little Johnny, "because it sure as hell wouldn't be a great loss, and it probably wouldn't be an accident either!"

PRINCESS PELOSI

A man was washed up on a beach after a terrible shipwreck, and aside from himself only a sheep and a sheepdog had survived.

After looking around he realized that they were stranded on a deserted island, and after being there awhile he got into the habit of taking his two animal companions to the beach every evening to watch the sunset.

One particular evening the sky was a fiery red with beautiful cirrus clouds, and the breeze was warm and gentle - a perfect night for romance. As they sat there the sheep started looking better and better to the lonely man, and soon he leaned over and put his arm around it - but the sheepdog, ever protective of the sheep, growled fiercely until the man removed his arm.

After that the three of them continued to enjoy the sunsets together, but there was no more cuddling. A few weeks passed by, and lo and behold there was another shipwreck of which the only survivor was Nancy Pelosi.

That evening the man brought Nancy to the sunset beach ritual. It was another beautiful evening - red sky, cirrus clouds, a warm and gentle breeze - perfect for a night of romance, and pretty soon the man started to get 'those feelings' again. He fought the urges for as long as he could but finally gave in and leaned over to Nancy and told her he hadn't had sex for months. Nancy batted her eyelashes and asked if there was anything she could do for him.

He said, "There sure is. Would you mind taking the dog for a walk?"

* * * * *

"Outgoing Speaker Nancy Pelosi gave a speech and handed the gavel to John Boehner. It was a very emotional moment for Pelosi, but she managed to keep a stiff upper lip... along with a tightly stretched forehead and unnaturally arched eyebrows." – Jay Leno

* * * * *

"Nancy Pelosi, who lost her position as Speaker of the House, says she will seek to become the House Minority Leader. And really, who is better qualified to be House Minority Leader than the person who led their party to becoming a minority in the first place." - Jay Leno

* * * * *

"For the first time in history, there are 100,000 home foreclosures in the month of September. 100,000 people were told this fall they were going to lose their house. 100,001, if you count Nancy Pelosi." – Jay Leno, the day after the 2010 mid-term elections

* * * * *

"Christine O'Donnell had a campaign ad where she said she's not a witch. Nancy Pelosi was furious. She said, "Hey, that's *my* slogan!"" – Jay Leno

* * * * *

"Nancy Pelosi said today we've waited 200 years for this. 200 years? How many face lifts has this woman had?" - Jay Leno

* * * * *

"The GOP picked up about 60 seats. It's the most new faces in Congress in over 50 years, if you don't count Nancy Pelosi's Botox treatments." – David Letterman

* * * * *

Nancy Pelosi's limo was traveling through the countryside when it hit and killed a cow. Nancy told the driver to go up to the farmhouse and tell the people living there what had happened.

After two hours the limo driver came back, obviously drunk, and with his shirt practically ripped off.

"What happened to you, and why were you gone so long?"' Pelosi demanded.

The driver said he went up to the farmhouse and told the family there what happened. The farmer's wife cooked him a fine meal, the farmer gave him some of the best moonshine he'd ever had, and then they sent him off to the barn for an hour with their beautiful twenty-something daughter.

Nancy asked, "What *exactly* did you tell them?"

The driver replied, "I told them that I was your driver, and that I had killed the cow…"

THE PEANUT FARMER

The Jimmy Carter Presidential Museum reopened this month after a major renovation that shifted emphasis to his post-presidency, since those were the years when he accomplished the most. After he dies there will no doubt be *another* renovation, to highlight how much more good he'll be accomplishing dead than while he was alive.

* * * * *

Johnny Carson, as *Carnac the Magnificent*, held up the envelope to his head and divined the answer – "Yes and no, pro and con, for and against." He then opened the envelope and read, "Describe Jimmy Carter's position on three major issues."

* * * * *

Former President Jimmy Carter went on a humanitarian mission to secure the freedom of Aijalon Mahli Gomes, who was sentenced to hard labor for illegally entering North Korea.

His aides say Carter didn't want to go unprepared and have to negotiate by the seat of his pants, so before leaving he spent hours with Rod Blagojevich, who is from Kim Jong's home state of "Ill" along with also being another windbag with a bad hairdo.

* * * * *

According to reports, Kim Jong-il wasn't in North Korea during Jimmy Carter's visit. Not good news for the world's most isolated, unpopular leader of all-time… and also not so good for Kim Jong-il.

* * * * *

Jimmy Carter arrived in North Korea to advocate the release of an American who is serving an 8 year sentence. Who better to negotiate than a man who is expert on nuts.

* * * * *

Q. Why did Jimmy Carter vote for Barack Obama?
A. Because Jimmy didn't want to be the worst President in history anymore.

* * * * *

In an open letter Jimmy Carter apologized for any words or deeds that may have upset the Jewish community. Unfortunately, he ended the letter by saying, "I wish all my Jewish friends a very Merry Christmas."

* * * * *

Jimmy Carter turned down an invitation by Brandeis University to debate professor Alan Dershowitz about Carter's book *Palestine: Peace not Apartheid*.

Carter told the *Boston Globe*, "I don't want to have a conversation, even indirectly, with Dershowitz."

That's Carterese for: "What? I'm not going to some Jewish university to talk about Israel with some Jew lawyer!"

* * * * *

Jimmy Carter and his wife had their bicycles stolen while vacationing in Florida. It is speculated the thieves were members of the Olympic triathalon squad in 1980.

* * * * *

Reports suggest that parts of former President Carter's new book may have been lifted from other books. Coincidentally, most of Barack Obama's presidency seems to have been copied from Jimmy Carter.

* * * * *

Bill Clinton, Al Gore and Jimmy Carter went to a fitness spa for some fun. After a nice lunch, all three decided to visit the mens' room where they found a strange-looking gent sitting at the entrance.

He said, "Welcome to the gentlemen's room. Be sure to check out our newest feature, a mirror that, when you look into it and say something truthful, will reward you with your wish. But be warned, if you say something false, you will be sucked into the mirror to live in a void of nothingness for eternity!"

The three men entered and upon finding the mirror, Bill Clinton stepped up and said, "I think I'm the most intelligent of us all," and he suddenly found the keys to a brand new Bentley in his hands.

Al Gore stepped up and said, "I think I'm the most ambitious of us all," and in an instant he was surrounded by a pile of money.

Excited over the possibility of finally having a wish come true, Jimmy Carter looked into the mirror and said, "I think...," and was instantly sucked into the mirror.

HOLLYWIERD

"Michael Moore, Mr. Controversy, is upset because his film *Fahrenheit 911* got an "R" rating for showing graphic footage. But to be fair, it *does* show a couple of close-ups of Michael Moore." - Craig Kilborn

* * * * *

"This week, our friend Al Franken is launching a new all liberal radio network called *Air America*. They say the purpose of *Air America* will be to balance out all the conservatives in the media, except, of course for NPR, CNN, CBS, ABC, NBC, and the *New York Times*." - Jay Leno

* * * * *

"Because the last election was such a disaster for the Democrats, it looks like the leader of the party might be stepping down. But enough about Barbra Streisand." - Jay Leno

* * * * *

"Michael Moore simultaneously represents everything I detest in a human being and everything I feel obligated to defend in an American. Quite simply, it is that stupid moron's right to be that utterly, completely wrong." – Dennis Miller

* * * * *

"The second type you have at these parades seems to be the (liberal) people who want to mislabel Hitler. Everybody in the world is Hitler. Bush is Hitler, Ashcroft is Hitler, Rumsfeld is Hitler. The only guy who isn't Hitler is the foreign guy with a mustache dropping people who disagree with him into the wood chipper. He's *not* Hitler." - Dennis Miller, describing how anti-war protesters call everyone but Hussein a Hitler

QUOTES SO STUPID THEY'RE FUNNY

"The WTC was not just an architectural monstrosity, but also terrible for people who didn't work there, for it said to all those people: 'If you can't work up here, boy, you're out of it.' That's why I'm sure that if those towers had been destroyed without loss of life, a lot of people would have cheered. Everything wrong with America led to the point where the country built that tower of Babel, which consequently had to be destroyed. And then came the next shock. We had to realize that the people that did this were brilliant. It showed that the ego we could hold up until September 10 was inadequate." - Norman Mailer

* * * * *

"I think that people like the Howard Sterns, the Bill O'Reillys and to a lesser degree the bin Ladens of the world are making a horrible contribution." – Sean Penn

* * * * *

"There is no terrorist threat in this country. This is a lie. This is the biggest lie we've been told." – Michael Moore

* * * * *

"I still want to be the candidate for guys with Confederate flags in their pickup trucks" - Howard Dean, apparently courting what he saw as the racist vote.

* * * * *

"I think the Confederate flag is a racist symbol."
– Howard Dean, a few days later.

* * * * *

"We've got to ask, why is this man (Osama bin Laden) so popular around the world? Why are people so supportive of him in many countries... that are riddled with poverty? He's been out in these countries for decades, building schools, building roads, building infrastructure, building day care facilities, building health care facilities, and the people are extremely grateful. We haven't done that. How would they look at us today if we had been there helping them with some of that rather than just being the people who are going to bomb in Iraq and go to Afghanistan?" - Democratic Senator Patty Murray

* * * * *

"If that had been *my* daughter, it wouldn't have taken an election to resolve it. It would have been up close and personal. We would have taken care of it real quick." - Cruz Bustamante talking about how he'd whomp Arnold Schwarzenegger good if "the Terminator" ever groped his daughter.

HINDSIGHT IS ALWAYS 20/20

Liberal hindsight about September 11th has degenerated to the level of barroom conversation.

"I didn't believe that the attack on the World Trade Center could have been prevented when we started this investigation," says Bob Kerrey, who has become de facto commission chairman. *"After studying the details for six months,* however, I now believe it could have been stopped."

After studying for six months, Kerrey could probably carry on a brief conversation in Farsi as well. But is that any proof that he could have read the future?

The most shameless (and for the purposes of this book, absurdly funny) meanderings came from Nicholas Kristof in the *New York Times.* "The 9/11 attacks could have been prevented," Kristof announced with admirable finality in a column entitled, "Why Didn't We Stop 9/11?" He then went on to imagine the conversation that should have taken place on August 6, 2001, after a CIA briefer informed President Bush that Osama Bin Laden was hoping to hit targets in America:

Bush: "Any idea where?"

C.I.A. briefer: "Sir, it could be almost anywhere, anytime. But pattern analysis suggest a target both huge and symbolic, perhaps another explosion to topple the World Trade Center, or the Sears Tower, or the Capitol. And Bin Laden has always looked for targets in aviation."

Bush: "Gosh. Hijacking airplanes?"

Briefer: "Yes, Mr. President, there are reports of a hijacking plot to ransom the blind sheik... or he could blow up planes and airports... in 1995... we let Philippine police interrogate [Abdul Jalm] Murad... a key figure in a plot to blow up as many as 12 United Delta and Northwest jumbo jets over the Pacific Ocean.. After he'd been beaten with chairs, burned with cigarettes and half-drowned, he disclosed a plan for a suicide airplane attack on the C.I.A.'s headquarters."

Bush: "You mean using a plane as a missile? If the Big Beard is into aviation, let's watch flight schools and airports."

And so forth.

All this reminds one of that old *New Yorker* cartoon where one barroom orator announces to another, "And how come we're not sending men to the moon anymore, either?" Rather than tutor these people, let's finish off Kristof's conversation for him:

Bush: "So who do you think Osama's got working for him here?"

Briefer: "Well, you know that Mohammad Atta guy down in Florida, the real surly one? We figure he's probably involved."

Bush: "Yeah, I never liked that guy."

Briefer: "He's living in Miami, but we figure that's a ruse. He'll probably hijack the plane somewhere up north, maybe around Boston."

Bush: "When do you think this thing will happen?"

Briefer: "They'll probably wait until September when people are back from vacation and the buildings are packed. Tuesdays are a slow flying day. They'll probably pick the first Tuesday in September."

Bush: "September 2nd? No, that's too close to Labor Day. It'll probably be September 11th."

Briefer: "That's a better guess."

Bush: "So let's go out and arrest him right now!"

Briefer: "Well, Mr. President, there's a problem. They haven't done anything wrong yet. The Fourth Amendment says you can't start investigating people until there's probable cause that they've committed or are about to commit a crime. All we've got now is that these guys are Middle

Easterners who've been taking flight lessons. If we try to move now, that would be racial profiling. You wouldn't want to do that, would you, sir?"

Bush: "Gosh no, I guess you're right."

Briefer: "So what do you want to suggest?"

Bush: "I've got it! They're going to hijack the plane out of Boston on September 11th, right? Let's take Air Force One and cruise the area that morning. As soon as we see a plane divert toward New York, well turn on our flashing lights, force them to land at Newark, read 'em their rights, and arrest them on the spot. That way we can stop the whole thing without violating the Constitution."

Briefer: (high-fiving) "Mr. President, you've got it! All system go! We"ll see you the morning of September 11th!"

It is sad that liberal Americans could be filled with so much hatred that they became "9-11 Truthers," and made themselves believe that an American President would either allow or engineer these heinous attacks, and that those same people would become indignant when Barack Obama's birth certificate was challenged. The only way to survive the vicious rhetoric of the left is to *keep laughing at them!*